◀ 1

PREFACE

The Belgians brew ... *etter believe it! Beer is hig* ... *say that it is to Belgium wl* ... *largest choice in styles and* ... *single country has more, and beer is considered food in Belgium. Actually, several gourmet dishes are prepared with Belgian beer: marinades, sauces, stews, soups, desserts ... Since the spectrum of taste is so much wider in beer, it makes perfect sense to choose a Belgian beer instead of wine with your next dinner!*

This book will guide you in your adventure discovering the rich history and choice of Belgian beer. You will find exceptional taste, beautiful flavors, centuries-old brewing recipes (some developed by monks), traditional craftsmanship, plenty of fun and pleasure while enjoying a healthy product.

At the beginning of this third millennium, we see a new growing quest for honest, traditional and 'slow' food products, and a focus on quality instead of quantity. Belgian beer is exactly that. A Belgian beer drinker drinks less but better. However, there is an important warning. A beer drinker discovering the Belgian beers is spoiled, there is no way back. He or she has discovered the Paradise of beers. Welcome!

Johnny Fincioen
President of the Global Beer Network

The author

Bernard Dubrulle, born December 9th 1974 in Charleroi. Graduated in Leisure and Tourism in Liège 1997.

With a particular interest in writing and tourism in its many forms, notably Belgium's special tourist attractions : folklore festivals, local products, ... and the beer for which his interest was born quite some time ago ..., he is the author of the Petit Futé for Charleroi, Pays de Sambre and Eau d'Heure.

The taster

Michel David was born January 18th, 1945. A graduate of the Ecole Hôtelière in Paris, he is the founder of the «Gambrinus Club» and of the «Ordre du Faro» He is also the co-founder, notably with Charles Fontaine and other brewers, of the BTB (Bières Traditionnelles Belges) «Belgian Traditional Beers» society. A gourmet who appreciates the pleasures of the table, Michel David is the author of several works about cooking with beer. He also preaches the association of an appropriate beer to a meal's various courses. An unlimited and inexhaustible collector of publicity materials, he is also present at numerous competitions and tastings, frequently as a member of the jury. For more than thirty years, Michel David has been an ardent and militant proponent of quality Belgian beers.

The Petit Futé on Belgian beers - Copyright registration 3rd trimester 2001
Editor : NEOCITY sprl - Geleytsbeek, 168 - 1180 Brussels Tel : 02 374 63 84 - Fax : 02 375 71 82 – e-mail : petitfute@wanadoo.be - Web : www.petitfute.com

Publication Director: Philippe Wyvekens
Author: Bernard Dubrulle
Beer taster: Michel David
Translation: Erik Poole and Isabelle Collard
Coordination: Stéphanie Grand
Administration: Marie Lasource
Illustrations: Cuirassé Portemine : Tel. 02 426 55 75
Composition: MK Partners sprl - 4260 Braives - Tel. 019 69 72 74
Photoengraving: Vreven sprl - 4257 Berloz - Tel : 019 33 87 87
Printing: Imprimeries Corlet - France
Distribution: Flammarion

Acknowledgments

To Charles Bamforth, Johan Blervacq, Catherine Bourlet, Fabienne Deshker, Pascal Hugue, Chantal Michel, as well as all the breweries that welcomed us and sent us information and photos. We must thank, in particular, Monsieur Jan De Brabanter of the Confederation of Belgian Brewers (CBB) for the help he graciously gave throughout the creation of this work, and Charles Fontaine whose generosity, good humour and brewing knowledge are all extraordinary arguments for the promotion of beer.

For the photographs : Collection R. Lanneau, Collection L. Decruyenaere, Collection Demecht, CBB, BSB, and the Boon, Bosteels, Haacht, Interbrew and Trois Fontaines breweries.

The Petit Futé was founded by Dominique Auzias (Nouvelles Editions de l'Université - Paris).

EDITORIAL

The beer market is undergoing a complete change. Tastes are evolving, new beers are created, small breweries spring-up in the North and South of the country. All this signals that the era when the great looting took place over the last decades, and saw so many small breweries close, has come definitely turned around.

This beer guide is composed of 4 parts:

– History: from the earliest history of beer up to the most recent methods of production and fermentation;

– How to undertake a tasting and the relationship between beer and food;

– A selection of 175 labels which are among the best representatives of the country and have had their physical and gustative properties decoded by our taster.

– Imbibing is good in theory, but its better in practice : a few ideas for brewing getaways and tourism : some breweries and museums to visit and a selection of good addresses where you can consume and where you can stock up.

Belgian beers are more than ever synonymous with diversity and quality. It represents flavour, tradition and rigour, the land, the table and of course, festivities, whether they are like Brueghel painted, a student gathering, surreal, intimate or even a town festival... We wish you now and in future, much pleasure in reading this guide and in the great discoveries that await.

TABLE OF CONTENTS

 Color of the beer 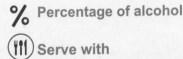 Percentage of alcohol
 Brewery (†\†) Serve with

"The John Martin's Finest Beers Selection":
An original range of special beers combining quality and tradition.
Developed with devotion since 1909 by the John Martin family business,
the selection puts the accent first on quality, then on diversity of
origin and strong individuality of taste.
From the John Martin's to the Gordon Finest Gold,
blond or dark, amber-coloured, fruity, sweet or slightly bitter,
the beers of the "John Martin's Selection" have always
fascinated beer lovers throughout the world.
We invite you to discover a unique range.
Taste and enjoy the experience.

A BIT OF HISTORY...

The evolution of beer from the beginning

The first known stage of more or less alcoholic beverages begins in the very earliest prehistoric times. It was a mixture of wild plants and honey, that is fermentable sugars, probably forgotten in the corner of a cave.

In Neolithic times, the wild plants were replaced by a mash of fermented barley. We can no longer talk of happenstance because there is a deliberate process followed by man.

Between 4000 and 3000 BC, this "technique" was im-proved little by little. Sumerians were the first to brew a mixture of barley and a variety of wheat, adding water to produce what is the ancient ancestor of barley beer. We can thereby braw a parallel between this "beer" and bread – the base of all foodstuffs – each composed of the same grains.

During the same period, Babylon was producing a light beer at harvest time named *bissebarussa*. This beverage was of course a thirst quencher, but also an offering to their gods and a form of salary to labourers.

The civilizations of South America, Africa and Asia each had

their own different fermented beverages made from local grains but these have no real correlation to beer and its derivatives.

The Egyptians, champions of the ancient world

By 2900 BC, the Egyptians already had veritable breweries, subject to strict regulation. They brewed a dozen different kinds of barley beer, of which some had high alcohol content and were flavoured with flowers and spices. The most widely known, and the only one whose name has survived into our time, was zythum. Mention is made of "barley wine" in this period as well. The Egyptians are also the first to have introduced into the mixture a syrup of fruits (probably dates) to keep their favourite drink from spoiling.

Little by little, barley beer made its entry onto the European con-

tinent. The earliest traces appeared in what is today Denmark, around 1500 BC, where a "beer" made from grains has been discovered.

In the Gauloise era, the principal drink was the famous barley wine, in addition to water and curdled milk. And, in regions where wine grapes would not grow and the Roman invasion could not introduce them, the inhabitants made barley beer or *cervoise* (of which Spanish has kept the root, giving *cerveza*). It is in this period that brewing families begin, and wooden barrels begin to replace pottery jugs. The early beginnings of Belgium's brewing history are here.

Throughout Europe, the phenomenon spread. Brewing sprang up everywhere, from the Caucuses to Scotland, passing through Germany where the inhabitants were already big consumers. The particular ingredients and flavours, each to its region, became well established. Wars themselves

played an important role as they brought the peoples and their brewing techniques into contact, albeit conflict.

The Prolific Middle Ages

In the VIIIth century, the monks of our abbeys, who had controlled for some time the art of brewing, became the first to use hops in a systematic manner. We can, from this time, refer to beer; fermented barley with the addition of hops. These ecclesiastics had in effect discovered the properties of the plant, to whit, increasing the period of preservation and inhibiting certain unwanted fermentation. We see also the appearance of the first true breweries, principally in the monasteries.

In the XIth century, the first brewers guild appeared in Affligem, in what is today the Brabant Flamand. Malt made its appearance in the brewing world as well. Essential for fermentation, it is barley, germinated then roasted.

The emergence of guilds and the setting of strict regulations are the major characteristics of the XIIth and XIIIth centuries. It is in this atmosphere that the city of Munich was founded and approximately 500 breweries appeared in "Germany." The Cistercian monks also took to the task, and the first Belgian monastic brewery was founded at Villers-la-Ville (Brabant Wallon), supplied with water from the local river (Thyle). The quality of this water plays its classic role even today in the production of the beer. And, since water was often un-potable except after boiling, we also see a principle reason for the daily consumption of a light beer, for children as well as adults.

The XVth century witnesses the definitive disappearance of barley beer and of *gruyt*, replaced by beer and hops. The most significant changes were in technique and quality. Breweries multiplied continually through the XVIth century.

In the XVIIth century the king of France granted to brewers a title of "juré" which gave them the right to brew. This was denied to cabaret or pub owners.

The system of guilds was abolished in the XVIIIth century, a century which elsewhere welcomed many new advancements, such as, in 1760 the introduction of the thermometer, and from 1784, the progressive replacement of *fourquets* (wooden stirring paddles) by steam powered equipment.

Thank you, Monsieur Pasteur...

The industrial revolution begun at the start of the XIXth century swept in a continuing modernisation and signalled the end of brewing in the old familial ways. In 1805 we see the introduction of the saccharometer, designed to measure and control the quantity of sugars.

But the most notable improvements are the discovery of yeast by Louis Pasteur and the development of industrial machinery. The isolation of the leavening cell, and the description of its fermentation properties gave new enlightenment to brewers. In 1883, the first pure culture of yeast was, besides, synonymous with consecration for French scientific efforts.

From the town of Pilsen in Bohemia (Czech Republic), another innovation was the invention of Pilsner, the first bottom fermented beer. This new type of beer was the result of the introduction of electricity into breweries. Pilsners must be brewed and fermented at very low temperatures. The brew masters could now produce beers of quality, consistency and stability. This discovery coincided with improvements in glass production techniques, which allowed inspection of the clarity and transparency of the Pilsner.

Modern developments

The XXth century has seen the appearance of radical changes in the manner of preservation of beer, as well as levels of production and consumption. A major characteristic is the disappearance of a considerable number of small breweries, for many reasons. One worth citing is the unquenchable thirst of the populace, through the seventies, for pilsners, which we have seen, require considerable investment in infrastructure. This investment was much too important for most of the 3,300 breweries located on the Belgian territory around 1900.

The first and second World Wars and the armies' demand for copper, the virulence of anti-alcoholic leagues, the crises of the thirties and seventies, and consolidation of smaller breweries by large multinational concerns are all additional causes of this disappearance.

Today, there remains only about 140 breweries in Belgium, but most are affiliates of larger brewing groups, which brings to just 80 the number of truly independent breweries, which produce the entirety of the 450 beers of Belgium.

End of the century momentum ...

However, all is not lost, quite the contrary. Since the 80's, several family run breweries have appeared, producing "special" type beers. Direct consequence of this upheaval: we no longer measure, in recent years, the number of barrels with unequalled quality, but rather with unequalled secrecy about their recipes. Specialists agree, for that matter, that in this particular category three new beers come along for every two that disappear.

The craze for "different" beverages corresponds to a notable shift in the Belgian lifestyle, and by extension all Europeans'. A steady rise in at-home consumption has been recorded, due in part to the phenomenon of *cocooning* and in part to the strict (and justified) prohibitions on driving under the influence of alcohol. These shifts have driven a search for products with marked differences and a greater sense of well-being and accommodation.

The hegemony of Pilsner over other beers seems then to have been weakened at the end of this century, even if, for the time being, it remains the preferred beverage for many of us, in terms of quantity consumed, at least!

THE STAGES OF MAKING

Making Beer

The Principle Ingredients

The Water

As strange as it may seem to some, water is indispensable to the making of beer . Water makes up at least 90% of the beverage's composition and its quality determines the beverage's quality, even if, as is now possible and some brewers do not hesitate to do, certain characteristics, most notably its ph, may be modified. In practice, there is no great beer without great water

at the start. In most cases, the water is taken from a source local to the brewery.

The Malt

After the water, malt is the basic ingredient of all beers. It is, principally, barley that is germinated then quickly dried (in brewing via roasting). Raw barley being insoluble in water, roasting and then grinding into a powder are necessary steps .

The duration and temperature of the roasting determine the colour and flavour imparted to the beer . During its germination and malting, the barley acquires a series of enzymes, useful in brewing, and transforms its indigestible starches into sugars available for assimilation . Some types of beer also use malt made from wheat, and notably the white beers and Pilsners also use rice and corn in their composition . According to the numbers, Germany and France are the top suppliers of barley in the world; our neighbours from the other side of the Quiévrain supply a full 10% of the cereal grains used in brewing.

The Hops

Called *the brewer's green-gold*, hops entered into brewing in the XIIth century and had completely re-placed competing spices by the XVth century. A climbing vine, it can reach a height of four or five metres, and live 100 years. It is the flower of the female plant (differing from the male plant) that interests the brewer . Their glands secrete an aromatic resin called lupulin. The essential oils and powder obtained from these glands give the perfume and bitterness necessary to each beer. Hops is also an excellent preservative and, thanks to its tannins, aids in clarifying the beer. Hops for brewing is cultivated in the temperate regions of Europe, the Americas and Oceania . The principle beer consuming countries are also the principal hops producing countries.

The Yeasts

Thanks to yeasts, single-celled micro-organisms that reproduce exponentially, the sugars in the mash of malt are transformed into alcohol and CO_2. In the XVIIIth century, the chemist Lavoisier, who most of us suffered through learning about in school, showed that the sugars burned during fermentation were equal to the additional gas and alcohol produced. This transformation takes place during the 6 to 10 days that follow the initiation of fermentation. There are two types of leavening yeasts : high and low. The high (or Ale type) yeasts are used for top fermented beers: they act above 20°C and rise to the surface when fermentation is complete. The low (or Lager type) yeasts are used for bottom fermented beers: they act below 10°C and drop to the bottom of the vat when fermentation is complete. When speaking of re-fermentation in the bottle, this refers to beer containing lees, that is, beer that carries some of its fermenting yeast with it into its bottle.

Hops flowers

Milling and Mashing

Mashing is, after the malting of the grains, the second process in making beer. The mixture of barley and sometimes malted wheat is ground then added to boiling water in a vat (the *tun*) and sometimes spices (coriander, orange rind, thyme, basil, genever, ...etc.) go in as well. The starches contained in the grains turn little by little into sugar and give birth to the mash, which will be filtered to remove any solid particles.

At this point, in a second vat (the *kettle* or *copper*), the brewer progressively warms the resulting mixture (the wort), thereby finishing the transformation of the residual sugars. He must continually stir the wort to avoid it sticking to the lining of the vat.

Next comes the addition of the hops (the hopping) at a temperature of +/- 70°C, then bringing the mixture to a boil again. The liquid is then quickly cooled (to about 20°C for a top fermentation and 8°C for a bottom fermentation).

The yeast then enters into the scene, in a well oxygenated vat to encourage fermentation, the duration of which depends on the type of beer being produced.

True or False

True : modern facilities use stainless steel for their brewing vats.

Most of those who still use copper vats do so only to retain the aesthetic for their visitors, the copper being simply an envelope around the stainless interior.

False : all fruit beers are made beginning with fresh fruit.

Many Lambics and other flavoured beers contain syrups or, still worse, synthetic essences.

True : bottled beer doesn't have the same flavour as beer from a keg.

In fact, the more conditioning that takes place in large volumes, the deeper the flavours and aromas. The augmentation of the flavour is therefore proportional to an increase in the volume of the container.

True and **False** : all Pilsners have identical flavour.

Certain pseudo-amateurs make their case very loudly, that each Pilsner has its own "gustative particulars." True, insofar as it concerns the private productions (Roman, Bavik, Martens,...), true also for Maes, which is non-pasteurised and presents a different character. But false for the three stars of the market sector (Jupiler, Stella, Primus) among which differentiation is practically impossible. It is only a question of affinity for one or another's region, the drinker identifying more easily with his own territory than that of a neighbour...

Fermentation

There are, in the diverse works on beer, different systems of classification, often according to the preference of the author. One can use the colour (blonde, brown, white, amber, ...), the production location, (Trappist, artisan, industrial), the country of production,.... But one criteria seems primordial : the type of fermentation.

In effect, the fermentation is what differentiates each beer from another because it determines the beer's look, flavour, perfume, taste and even consistency of the head. Beers can therefore be classified in three distinct categories, which are bottom fermentation, top fermentation and spontaneous fermentation. Each of which is divisible into sub-categories.

The type of fermentation is determined by the strain of yeast used, the temperature of brewing, the position of the yeast in the vat and the duration of the fermentation.

Bottom Fermented Beers

The principle characteristics of a bottom (or low) fermentation are : fermentation at a low temperature (6 to 14°C), clouds of yeast that fall

Pre-war village pub

techniques discovered just at the end of the XIXth century. Since then, through no real effort of its own, it has driven a series of other beers into oblivion. And although it seems to be slowing slightly in recent times, due to specialty beers being drunk in higher quantities than ten or twenty years ago, it still leads the pack and is the preferred beer of Belgians in terms of litres consumed.

Non- or Low-Alcohol Beers

Initiated by Tourtel (Kronembourg) and the famous barman Paul, the non- or low-alcohol beer movement was rapidly adopted by other breweries. A true alternative for those who do not wish or can not consume alcohol (for ethnic of medical reasons, as well as a teetotalling evening) they are made by the same methods as traditional Pilsners, with the sole resulting difference being a less extended fermentation (to maintain lower alcohol levels) and therefore, necessarily, a less pronounced flavour. We can place in the same category the "table beers" (Piedboeuf, Maes Nature, ...), even though their use and philosophy diverge from the N.A. (Non-Alcoholic) efforts. These are often consumed at mealtime thanks to their light character and digestive properties.

to the bottom of the vat and a fermentation over a period of 6 to 8 days. The strains of yeast used are *Saccharomyces uvarum* or *Saccharomyces carlsbergensis*.

The Pilsners

Pilsner is the all-around beer. It is the most produced and most consumed in the world, and the largest international breweries are essentially based on this type of beer. Pilsners star at large scale festivals like Oktober Fest in Bavaria, and are the ubiquitous companion at student gatherings throughout Belgium. Refreshing, thirst-quenching and low in alcohol, a drinker can stick with it over a long period without causing too much damage.

Helping along its wide popularity, it is considered by a large number among us to be an excellent beer to accompany daily meals, as an alternative to wine or "table beer". But, a lesser-known fact about Pilsner is that it is above all a "modern" beer since it is produced using

Top Fermented Beers

The principle characteristics of a top (or high) fermentation are: fermentation at a high temperature (18 to 32°C), clouds of yeast that form fro~~th~~ at the top of the vat and a mentation over a period of 4 to 6 days. The strain of yeast used is the *Saccharomyces cerevisiae*.

Trappists

"Trappist" beer is considered the royal category of beer by many amateurs. Since 1962, this ap-

pellation is officially granted and corresponds to a simple rule : the brewing must be performed by Trappist monks, in an abbey of that order. Until recently there were five in Belgium and one in the Netherlands, the Trappe of Koningshoeven. But, in 1999 this last member saw its appellation revoked because the brewing was no longer per-formed entirely within the ab-bey. In contrast, a tiny new one sprang up, in Achel, in the prov-ince of Limbourg, making Bel-gium the exclusive world home of the appellation. Since 1997, the Trappist beers have united under the label " Authentic Trappist Product ". This associa-tion certifies the origin of the products (beer but also cheeses, biscuits, ...), the conditions of

production, and the return of a portion of the proceeds from their sale to works of a social character.

Abbey Beers

Confusion is common, and it bears repeating : Abbey beers are not Trappist and vice versa. Abbey beers, though sometimes made from ancient recipes held my monks, are produced by in-dependent breweries (Leffe by Interbrew, Tongerloo by Haacht, ...). In contrast to Trappists, the religious commu-nity does not enter, in any way, into the production or distribu-tion of these beers, though they may receive royalties. The reci-pes are sometimes original, sometimes adaptations, but usually these are beers, how-ever created, that take their name from an actual or histori-cal abbey, which licensed the name to an industrial brewery, without respect to whether the abbey in question had any his-tory of brewing.

In the last few years, a new cat-egory of Abbey beers has ap-peared. These are beers produced by a private brewery, installed within the confines of an abbey deserted by its origi-nal occupants in the past (Abbaye des Rocs at Montignies-sur-Roc, Abbaye d'Aulne at Gozée, ...).

White Beers

Refreshing, is without a doubt the best qualification of these beers which owe their name to their cloudy state and light, though slightly yellow, colour. Endowed with a relatively small amount of alcohol, they are also characterised by a high

> A white beer should be served and drunk in 7 (seven) minutes, after which oxidation will take its toll.

quantity of wheat. It is the wheat, un-malted, that gives them their pale colour and lightly fruity flavour, their cloudy state being due to the still-active yeast, providing the second fermentation in the bottle.

White beer (*witbier* or *tarwebier* in Dutch), though very popular in recent times, is a very old beer, of which we find traces as far back as the Middle Ages. Little by little, with the development of more and more modern techniques, White Beers began to disappear from the brewing landscape until they reached a point of almost total neglect after the Second World War. No one counted on the tenacity of one Pierre Célis, a dairyman, who, on a warm evening in the summer of 1964, decided to re-launch this type of beer.

Nowadays, several breweries have reinstated it to a place of honour, the most famous being Hoegaarden. It is one of the largest categories of beer exported outside our borders and is consumed above all by the young and women, who it pleases with its thirst-quenching character. In another style, the Huyghe brewery, known primarily for its *Delirium Tremens*, developed an array of white beers low in alcohol and, above all, infused with flavours (strawberry, passion fruit, chocolate, cherry, honey,...).

The "Ales"

This term, of English origin, encompasses the amber coloured beers (from the lightest to the most sombre) and of a volume of alcohol close to the standard value (5%). Generally thirst-quenching, they often have a solid character. Far from being the best represented category of beer in Belgium (it is much better represented in Great Britain where it is the specialty), there are nonetheless a few excellent examples.

> Each year at Hoegaarden, the Grietmuilviering takes place, a sumptuous celebration during which they bury a cask of Blanche.

The Flemish Browns

Also known as old browns (" Oud bruin "), and in French " Rouges Flamands " or "Flemish Reds", these beers also belong to a category of which Belgium is the exclusive world home. What's more, their region of production is limited to Flanders. Like the Lambics (see below), they too use spontaneous fermentation and are aged in wooden casks (which impart to them a good deal of their character). But the peculiarity about these beers, other than their typical colour, is the balancing of top fermentation and spontaneous fermentation. Often low in alcohol, they are distinguished by their bitter-sweet (but not acid) taste and their thirst-quenching properties.

Sometimes, certain breweries mash cherries into the brew, in keeping with the philosophy of the "krieks" from the region of Brussels.

The others

In this chapter, we cover many beers with different characters, whether due to their flavour, level of alcohol, region of production, colour, etc. One might think that they belong to no category. In reality, they are all placed in a category known as "Belgian Specials", a bit of a catch-all, but distinguished by the fact that these beers are found only in Belgium.

The spontaneously fermented

Historically, before the discovery of yeasts by Louis Pasteur, beers fermented spontaneously, in contact with the surrounding air. Today they all add yeasts, either top or bottom fermenting. All? No! A small part of the world still resists the invasion. This resistance is situated in Belgium, more precisely, the area to the south and west of Brussels, in a region called the *Pajottenland* – argot from *Pajot* (patriot) or a dialectical adaptation of the word "mortier" (mortar). In this small corner of Belgium, they say the air is very special, and favours the development of certain types of cells. These micro-organisms, in coming in contact with the mash, cooling in its containers, trigger fermentation and give lambic its special flavour, crisp and lightly acid.

Natural leaveners are numerous in lambics : there are no less than 86 identified species. The most important are named *Brettanomyces bruxellensis* and *Brettanomyces lambicus*. These yeasts are in effect the "responsible parties" for the assimilation of the sugars not yet broken down, resulting in the very low sugar content of Lambics.

Lambic

Up until the beginning of the century, Brussels and its region had hundreds of breweries that produced Lambic. Today, at the opening of the third millennium, there are only two in the Capital of Europe, and in the entire region the number only reaches about a dozen.

Lambic, which takes its name from Lembeek in the Brabant Flamand, is the base of all the Gueuzes, Krieks and their derivatives. Created from an ancestral recipe (dating from Roman times according to some, while others point to documentation ancient enough from the XVIth century), Lambic is composed of +/-65% malted barley and +/-35% un-malted wheat. It is brewed with heirloom hops, aged 2 to 3 years, to play the role of a preservative. During its " cooking ", lasting 6 hours, a portion of the aged

Fermenting lambic

hops is added. It is brewed in the winter months (October to March) since the air-borne micro-organisms are free of harmful bacteria during this time.

After it is mashed, the open fermentation vats are exposed to the ambient air via holes pierced in their covers. Difficult to drink in this state, due to its high acidity, the Lambic matures for a period (from several weeks up to three years) in wooden casks before appearing in our glasses. Contrary to most other beers, Lambic forms absolutely no head and is often served in small straight-sided glasses. Even if, as the years go by, its popularity with the people of Brussels and Belgium continues to fall, it is being bolstered by a rising success abroad.

The brewer must wait, with only very rare exceptions, a minimum of one year before obtaining a beer destined to serve as the base for another product like a Gueuze or Kriek.

Faros

Faro is a light beer (also produced in the winter), made from Lambic with too high an acid content to be drunk and water ; this is sweetened with sugar syrup. A very fine specialty of Brussels, Faro was popular in the time of Breughel. As in other cases, the appearance of bottom fermented beers sounded the death knell for this traditional beer, although the recent resurgence of interest in specialty breweries has allowed it to reappear in our taverns. It must be drunk while young, and keeps for no more than a couple of weeks. The principle producers

are : Boon, Cantillon, De Troch, Lindemans and Timmermans.

Gueuze

Nicknamed the " champagne of Brussels ", Gueuze is an assemblage of Lambics of different ages and characters. During the mixture, the unassimilated sugars of the younger beers provoke a second fermentation of the whole, which when exhausted, leave tiny " champagne " bubbles, creating an entirely different beverage. Lambics of three to five different vintages are required to produce a good Gueuze. As a short history, consider that this beer takes its name from the Gueux, during the reign of Philippe II. Gueuze is particularly appreciated when accompanying specialties of Brussels like a tartine of white cheese, or fine herbs, or with *croques monsieur*. It is also one of the only beers available for diabetics because it is completely free of sugars.

Addition of the cherries to the lambic

The beer is put into barrels for shipping.

Kriek and other Fruit Lambics

Kriek is prepared from young Lambic and fresh cherries "from the north" (originally coming from Schaerbeek near Brussels), mashed into the oak casks and giving the beer a beautiful reddish colour. For the preparation, a minimum of 50 kg of fruit is required per 250 litres of Lambic. The raspberry and, to a certain degree blackcurrant, are produced in a similar manner but with slightly more fresh fruit than for the Kriek. One must note however, that brewers are falling back more and more on natural essences (or even synthetic essences) resulting in not necessarily the same flavours. This procedure is almost ubiquitous in the production of those other than the cherry and raspberry.

Another important note, a true Kriek is prepared with a base of only Lambic, which signifies that the region of production should respect the same geographical limits as for the Lambic. Certain Flemish browns use the term " kriek " (see elsewhere), although they are merely top fermented beers infused with a cherry essence.

Bottling assembly line

Maturation

Conditioning the beer

The beer, once having reached this stage, is again transferred, and filtered, into another vat, or sometimes returned to the same vat in which it was fermented. Over the next several weeks, it will refine its flavour while resting at a temperature close to zero degrees. This process allows the liquid to clarify and also to gain a better saturation with CO_2. During this last stage of production, the beer acquires its digestive qualities and undergoes a second fermentation. It is for this reason that we must logically speak of triple fermentation if a beer undergoes re-fermentation in the bottle.

A last transfer, vats receive the beer destined to be pasteurised.

Dispensing the beer

The dispensing into bottles, kegs or cans, known as drawing-off or racking, is a step less innocuous than it would seem . It requires that the beer retain the properties it has acquired throughout its brewing and fermentation (saturation with carbon dioxide gas, important to the head, un-touched by outside contaminants ... etc.).

Dispensing into bottles or kegs, previously cleaned and disinfected, as well as dispensing into cans, must be done in great haste and be executed, in the majority of cases, by an automated apparatus . Regulation states that the beer must never come in contact with air before being consumed . This explains why kegs, after being re-filled, are automatically weighed to the greatest degree of precision possible . Any discrepancy in weight leads to discarding the keg concerned.

For transportation

Old pewter tankard

Packaging beer in metal (kegs and cans), which first appeared in the 30s, took off when tin was abandoned as a container material. Actually, the interior

Cigar or Dessert ?

A recent test, conducted at the initiative of a magazine specialized in beer, concerning the marriage between different types of Havanas and some types of special beers, gave the conclusions that follow. The beers that go best with a Havana are browns (Doubles), rich and possessing a high level of alcohol. The explanation seems simple enough : the aromas of the two products combine ideally : we find in each chocolate, leather, coffee, roasting and... some notes of smoke. The strength of the beer impedes the pungent wisps of the cigar from covering its own aromas.

of the container is covered with a glaze that inhibits the beer from absorbing a metallic flavour. This conditioning is regularly used for all products destined for export : it avoids exposure to too much light and allows for a higher usable volume than glass.

The classic volumes for bottles are 25cl, 33cl, 37,5cl, 75 cl et 1,5l. The more modern kegs hold 30l or 50l and cans 33cl and 50cl. Recently, Stella Artois (Interbrew) has become available in tankers of 200 litres.

Conservation

Keeping bottles at home should be done in a cellar or at least in a dark room with a constant temperature of 10 to 14°C . Only certain beers (those bottom fermented) can be stored at a lower temperature before being consumed . But, in all cases, beer should never be stored too long in a refrigerator This runs the risk of removing some of the beer's qualities, mostly of the flavour . It is suggested that beer be placed in a refrigerator only a few hours before it is to be consumed.

As for the position of the bottles, it is essentially a question of the type being used. Those bunged with a cork are normally stored standing, opening at the top, whereas those corked like champagne are inclined 45, opening to the top. When they are stored laying on their side, the beer has greater contact with the lees in the bottle, and the flavour is more fully developed. Take note that beer as good or even perfect as it may be, can never be stored as long as wine. It is therefore suggested that they be drunk as quickly as possible, except for those that are bottled fermented, which may withstand longer storage (years in some cases). Lastly, certain beers are bottled before their ripening is complete : one must wait a few months before they develop the flavour the brewer intended them to have.

UNDERTAKING A BEER-TASTING SESSION

FOAMY HEAD, OAKY AROMA, DISTINCT MELTING SOURNESS, WARM GOLDEN COLOR,.... HICCUP!...GOOD CARBONATION..

BURP!!

Although beer drinking goes back to the twilight of recorded time, the discovery of its different qualities and characteristics is much more recent. Tasting, in its official sense, and the pleasures of the same, has really just started and gains new converts on a daily basis.

To taste a beer is to understand and appreciate a beer. It is above all, as in wine tasting, to receive a series of "messages" that the drink has to give you. It is therefore imperative to follow a set of rules that, though they may sometimes appear to be "academic", are nonetheless essential.

To sum up, one must appreciate the difference between "drinking beer" and "beer tasting". This is learned, like all lessons, over time. Here are several ways to gain an appreciation of this fine beverage.

What beer in which glass?

The theory behind...

A drinker, novice or expert, uses at least three of his five senses when tasting beer : sight, smell and taste. For these senses to be used fully, it is important to start with the appropriate glass. One could almost say that each beer has its own glass, even though in most cases, the glasses are simply an adaptation of one of the four basic designs used currently (chalice, tulip, flute and straight-sided pilsner) which best serves the image the brewery wants to impart to its product.

The glass must be completely clean (any trace of oils or foreign objects will "kill" the beer immediately), washed by hand, and if possible, dried in the open air. The use of dishwasher should be prohibited since the detergents hinder the formation of a good head, and can make the beer flat (we know it from experience). It is also suggested that the glass be rinsed with clean water before pouring the beer to permit the head to expand freely.

... the practice

One would therefore look for the "queen" of beers, the Trappists, to be served in a "chalice" to allow the aroma to be better appreciated. The head expanding over a larger surface develops a stronger, more marked bouquet.

Abbey beers, the ambers and most "special" beers, are more appropriately served in a "tulip" glass. This helps to build and maintain a better head and to more slowly diffuse the aroma. If need be, one could also serve a Trappist in this style of glass.

Beers with a crisp, strong aroma, for instance the Krieks and other fruit Gueuzes, are better served by a flute, tall and slightly flared. The small surface exposed to the air concentrates the subtle perfumes and slows the release of CO_2.

Pilsner and its derivatives show-off their clarity and bubbly nature best in a straight-sided glass without a foot. Slightly flared, this glass preserves the head for the same reasons as the tulip, and better presents the beer's strong nose of fresh hops. For that reason, try drinking a Pilsner from a chalice...

What beer at what temperature ?

Here, the rules are less strict than for the type of glass. The service temperature for a beer also depends on each individual's taste.

Note that in general, beer does not do well in cold conditions, except for the bottom fermented beers where it is an essential element, both in its production and in its consumption. Pilsners can therefore be appreciated between 3 and 8°C, which highlights their thirst quenching qualities. The white beers are an exception from the top fermentation category since they are also most agreeable under 10°C.

To your good health, kids!

The enemy came from the cold

Cold being the eternal enemy of the top fermented beers, from brewing through tasting, most of them are best consumed at "cellar temperature" (10 to 14°C). The complexity of the aromas are better revealed. Otherwise, the more complex a beer's flavour and aroma, the more preferable it is to be drunk at a higher temperature. As for the spontaneously fermented beers, they follow the same rules as the others : from 12 to 14°C for the Gueuzes and from 6 to 8°C for the Lambics and fruit Gueuzes.

To further improve the tasting, it is best to retrieve the beers from the cellar a few minutes before serving in order to allow them to "acclimatize" themselves to the ambient temperature. No beer should spend too long in the refrigerator, even those that are to be served cold, since this runs the risk of de-stroying some of their properties and undoing the work of the yeasts. Try then, to chill your Pilsners one or two hours before drinking and remember that the higher the alcohol content, the higher the appropriate serving temperature.

How to serve a beer ?

After determining the correct glass to use and the desired service temperature, one must then pour the beer in the proper manner. Though the act seems fairly innocuous, it is best performed, once again, according to a few simple principles. One last time, it is preferable that the glass be slightly moist, especially for the bottom fermentation beers. Also, do not forget to underline the importance of the head. It holds a series of special aromas that would surely be a pity to miss.

To obtain a good "head" of foam of +/- 3 centimetres, one

must pour the beer rapidly but not in a brisk motion, into the middle of a glass inclined at 45°, slowly pitched back upright after it is filled halfway and finished by pouring the last of the beer while raising the bottle away from the glass. Avoid as much as possible pouring the beer directly into the glass while resting the bottle's neck on the rim.

A better pour than you thought

Not all beers foam in the same manner. The foam is like a barometer of the quality and type of beer. A Lambic hardly foams at all and the head disappears as quickly as the liquid is poured, while the top fermentation beers give abundant, creamy and persistent foam.

Another observation concerns those beers that undergo a second bottle fermentation. These often have a deposit of yeast, the quantity depending on their age, at the bottom of the bottle. Ideally for these beers, they should rest upright for 48 hours before serving, in order to avoid serving a beer full of yeast particles.

One might also serve the beer keeping the bottle horizontal and pouring out the deposits for tasting but the clarity will most certainly be affected. This point is very much a question of taste, since the lees are the component of beer with the most vitamins (notably vitamin B).

Its worth a look...

During the observation phase, the drinker should linger over the "external" characteristics of the beer. One should analyse the colour of the brew, due in large part to the degree of roasting or kilning of the malt and the texture of the head.

The head is generally white, sometimes light brown if the liquid it tops is very dark. One should also watch for the longevity of the head (stability or rapid dissolution), its structure, that is, the size of the bubbles and their compactness, as well as its texture. In the case of beers that are re-fermented in the bottle and White Beers, the foam is very thick, principally due to the use of wheat at the moment of brewing. Finally, an expert taster can also add other elements to the list, like the adherence of the foam to the sides of the glass.

As for the beer itself, one should note its bubbles, clarity and of course, colour.

Preparation phase (turning the glass)

Each beer has its own specific aromas. For them to be fully released, they must come into contact with the oxygen in the ambient air. For this reason, it

is preferable to wait a few seconds before serving a freshly poured beer (this allows time for the exchange of CO_2 and oxygen). In addition, to ensure fuller exposure to the air, one should make small concentric circles with the glass. This gesture, which can appear odd, or even ineffective, is actually crucial because a beer that is well oxygenated will have a different flavour, more like the one intended by the brewer.

Breathing phase

Things happen little by little. Beer, like any other alimentary product, liquid or solid, is characterised by the base flavours (sweet, salt, acid, bitter), the only ones discernable by the taste buds, and by other more subtle aromatics (spices, flowers, fruits, ...) that the nose, and only the nose, can appreciate in the correct manner. These aromatics, and the scents that they produce, are called the bouquet or "nose". It is therefore very important to

This plaque usually guarantees a properly served beer

instil in oneself, by way of a healthy sniff, the aromas and odours that each beer releases, in addition to its perfumes of hops, malt or yeast. It is also a way to "whets one's appetite". This operation should be done fairly quickly, as the delicate aromas do not linger.

Tasting phase

Beer is tasted in small mouthfuls, rolled around the interior of the mouth, and above all, while continually bringing it in contact with oxygen. For this, one must draw a small amount of air into the mouth to bring it into contact with the beer. The impregnation of the taste buds is what determines the taste of the beer, and this can also leave a thin film on the tongue. Exhaling through the nose, while the liquid is still in the mouth, raises aromas to the rear of the nose carrying new flavours. Finally, after the beer is swallowed, the flavours that remain in the mouth and on the tongue constitute the after-taste, fleeting and light, or heavy and persistent. To define it, it is said to linger in the mouth. The after-taste receives its influences from the degree to which the hops was dried, and from the body of the beer (texture and aroma).

The purity law or Reinheitsgebot

In 1516, the powerful Bavaria, whose brewing empire already shined, instated a law that forbade the introduction into beer of any ingredient other than water, hops, barley, and later, yeast. Some who were more « lax » allowed wheat. Fundamentally good, since it reduced the risks of contaminating beer with foreign materials, it spread rapidly throughout Europe. And, over time, as techniques evolved allowing the introduction of other ingredients in a viable manner (one of the Belgian examples being the addition of cherries to Lambic to produce Kriek), the Germans still stuck to this law, despite wind and tide. What would have seemed an internal problem now took on an international dimension, because Germany took advantage of this law, entrenching itself behind it and allowing no foreign beers to be imported which did not respect the Reinheitsgebot. The European Court of Justice ruled in favour of other beer producing countries (of which Belgium is one) and demanded that Germany change this antiquated law, more than 450 years old.

BEER IN CUISINE

In Belgium, beer has always been intimately associated with cuisine. To be convinced, one has only to look at the number of dishes, often regional, that incorporate beer (blond or brown), gueuze, kriek or even trappist. Beer enters into the composition of these dishes either as a principle ingredient (Beef stew, rabbit à la gueuze,...) or as a sweetener, softener or fermenting agent (in waffles for example).

For some time, beer has also been included as a part of the meal, as an accompanying beverage. It's no longer just a pilsner or a table beer, drunk along with your everyday meal, but rather the association of specific beers with specific dishes, exactly as for wine.

What beer with which dish ?

From appetizer to dessert

Beer has broken in amongst the numerous other gastronomic ingredients. But, from the dietetic point of view, the more orthodox remain reticent. Although, in equal volumes, beer is less caloric than wine, and the alcohol it contains evaporates immediately during cooking. Less alcoholic than wine, it is also considered a better aid to digestion among many amateurs.

So, it is completely possible to create an entire meal of these dishes, elaborate or not, based on beer, accompanied by different "vintages", from the aperitif to the dessert, and why not ... to the night-cap !

In as much as it is an ingredient in a dish, beer is an excellent enhancer of flavour, it also gives better balance to sauces and brings with it additional flavours (spices), by the simple fact that these things do not evaporate away during cooking. Visually, beer is also a good colouring agent ... and therefore popular with everyone who "eats with their eyes!"

Simmered dishes like all the beers

To contrast or to complement

Three different manners of associating a beer with the dish it accompanies can be proposed: as a re-enforcement, as a compliment or as a contrast, among the four base flavours (acid, bitter, sweet, salt).

In the first case, the easiest to accomplish, the intent is to associate two identical flavours (example : bitter – bitter, endive – pilsner ; sweet/fruit – sweet/fruit, kriek – cherry sorbet, ...).

In the second case, a little more difficult to do, the intent is to combine complimentary flavours, while maintaining a certain balance (classic example : acid/salt – acid/sweet, shrimp – Rodenbach).

Mussels, French fries and... a Pils beer: a great classic!

Far more difficult, and in our opinion something reserved for professionals, the third case permits the confrontation of two opposite tastes (acid and bitter, for example). Clearly, this gives much more liberty to the "sommelier" and, on the condition that the beer does not mask the flavour of the dish (and vice versa), there are innumerable combinations available, more so limited by the particular tastes of the guests than any well defined rule.

To be sure, the best way not to make an error is to match a beer to a dish according to their geography. You will then be certain of making the ideal combination.

A last remark regarding beer consumption as an aperitif : one should be vigilant in ensuring that it is neither too strong in character, nor too high in alcohol so as not to perturb the taste buds for the following meal.

Associating beer and cheese

Belgium is home to an impressive number of different beers, and cheese is equally well represented throughout Belgium. Without a doubt it is for this reason that they marry so well, and have for such a long time. In both cases, we find local prod-

ucts. Perhaps it is also for this reason that the geographical association of beers and cheeses works in such a marvellous way : is it necessary to remind anyone about the excellent trappist cheeses... ?

For a beer and a cheese to fully support one another's flavours, it is best if the flavours "understand" one another ... it is better to avoid peculiar pairings. Don't forget that brown beers are always a little sweet, and blond beers are often more full-bodied (especially the "specials").

In short, a cheese with a light, fresh flavour, would go with beers of a lower alcohol content while a beer high in alcohol, with a pronounced, strong flavour, would go better with a strong, flavourful and savoury cheese.

Some regional recipes

Since Belgium is composed of very different regions, it follows that the disparities would be reflected in the cuisine. And since the Belgians have, since the far-

thest back reaches of time, practised the art of eating well, it shouldn't surprise you to find that recipes involving beer have traversed the ages and become famous throughout the territory. As for today's culinary landscape, it is speckled more and more with the arrival of new venues, launching themselves, often with success, into the grand adventure that is cooking with beer. They are herewith thanked.

Flanders

Risotto of asparagus with sea perch and scallops St-Jacques à la De Koninck

Serves four:

12 asparagus, 80g of Arborio rice, 80g brunoise of carrot (diced), 80g brunoise of zucchini, 1 bottle of De Koninck, 1dl cream, pepper and salt, 4 filets of sea perch (with the skin on) of 80g each, 4 scallops Saint-Jacques, 1dl chicken or poultry stock, a few pieces of chilled butter.

Clean the asparagus and cook it until tender. Reserve 3cm of each spear head and dice the remainder of the spear. Keep warm.

Cook the rice and add the brunoise of carrot, zucchini, and diced asparagus. Give the mixture a healthy splash of the De Koninck, add the 1dl of cream and re-heat to an appropriate temperature. Salt and pepper to taste.

Cook the perch filets, skin side down in a non-stick pan with a little butter and do the same with the scallops Saint-Jacques. Salt and pepper to taste, and keep warm.

For the sauce, reduce by half the 1dl of De Koninck and the 1dl of chicken or poultry stock, then bind it with several pieces of cold butter. Salt and pepper to taste.

Place the risotto on four warm plates. Add the asparagus tips, the perch filets and lastly the scallops Saint-Jacques. Decorate the plate as you wish.

Recipe from Freddy Debecker – "Eyckerhof" restaurant in Bornem

Duck breast in velour sauce

Serves four:

4 duck breasts, 1 litre veal reduction, 1 bottle of Charles Quint beer, 1 tablespoon brown sugar, 50g pâté de foie gras, pepper and salt, brown roux

Cook the duck breasts and keep them warm. In the interval, heat the veal reduction along with half the bottle of beer, add the sugar and salt and pepper to taste.

Next, incorporate the pâté de foie gras and mix until a homogenous mixture is formed. Thicken the mixture with the roux, and reduce before adding the remaining half of the beer, salt and pepper to taste, then keep the sauce warm.

Serve with potato rounds, golden delicious apple and young mushrooms.

Recipe from Arnould Mario – "Brasserie Savarin" restaurant in Gand

In Wallonie
Kidneys à la Chimay

Serves four:

800g veal kidneys, 100g de flour, 50g butter, 30cl veal reduction, 30cl Chimay, 4 tablespoons course ground mustard, 1 egg yolk, 25cl crème fraîche.

Clean and slice the kidneys into thin slices. Flour each slice and cook in butter, two minutes each side. Salt and pepper to taste.

Pour the Chimay into a deep skillet and reduce over a gentle heat. Add the veal reduction and reduce again. Mix the mustard, egg yolk and crème fraîche. Add this mixture to the sauce. Test the seasoning.

Reheat the kidneys in the sauce for two minutes, over low heat, before serving. Accompany with sautéed apple.

Recipe available on the Chimay Brewery web site.

Veal shoulder à la Chouffe

Serves four

600g boned veal shoulder, 2 onions, 200g leek whites, 200g carrot, 2 cloves garlic, 1 sprig of thyme, 1 sprig rosemary, 2 tablespoons sunflower oil, 2 tablespoons butter, 4 tablespoons crème fraîche, 40cl "Chouffe", 1 tablespoon chopped parsley, salt and pepper.

Cut the veal shoulder into 3 or 4 centimetre pieces. Peal and chop the onions, garlic, leek and carrots. Heat the oil and butter in a casserole. Add the veal pieces and brown on all sides. Add the onions, garlic, leek, carrots, thyme, rosemary and 30cl of "Chouffe".

Simmer covered for 50 minutes. Afterwards, remove the thyme and rosemary sprigs. Add the remaining beer and reduce the sauce over high heat. Add the crème fraîche.

Serve with mashed potatoes or croquettes, sautéed celery and broccoli. Garnish with chopped parsley.

Brussels
Beef Roulades au lambic

Serves four:

4 beef roulades, 1 large onion, 30cl of lambic, 20cl beef stock, 1 bouquet garni, 2 tablespoons lard or butter, salt, pepper, nutmeg.

Peel and finely chop the onion. Brown the chopped onion and roulades, three minutes on each side, in the sizzling lard. Salt, pepper and cover with a mixture of the lambic and beef stock.

Add the bouquet garni, and a healthy pinch of freshly ground nutmeg,

Cheers, to your health!

What are the nutritional properties of beer ? What is its influence on weight ? Is beer, overall, good or bad for your health ? Between popular theories and scientific research, the concerned consumer sometimes hesitates. Here are some statements taken from a very serious study, lead by two medical doctors, Jaak Janssens and the very charming Marleen Finoulst, and published in "Le Journal du Brasseur" (The Brewer's Journal).

"A beer that is low in alcohol can aid in the production of milk during pregnancy".

"Moderate beer consumption protects the heart and blood vessels".

"A cold soda contains two times more calories than a blond beer".

"Moderate beer drinkers shouldn't worry about gaining weight because of this drink".

"Beer has a diuretic effect".

"Beer contains no fats, very little protein, and a small amount of sugars. (...) it does not cause weight gain as some wrongly accuse. What's more, beer contains neither cholesterol nor dioxin (...)."

"With moderate consumption, beer can provide a contribution to vitamin needs."

"Alcohol does not compensate for the injurious effects of tobacco."

"(...) persons suffering from diabetes who consume a few glasses of alcoholic beverages recognize a lowered risk of premature death."

"The phenomenon of "beer belly" is above all due to the over-consumption of salty and fatty snacks that often accompanies the consumption of beer with heavy drinkers."

cover and simmer 1 hour over a gentle flame.

Sprinkle with chopped parsley and serve hot with potatoes, mashed or steamed.

To strengthen the sauce, one tablespoon of tomato concentrate may be dissolved in the lambic.

Veal balls à la bière blonde

Serves four :

500g ground veal, 200g onions, nutmeg, 5cl vinegar, 25cl blond beer, salt and pepper.

Make small balls from the ground veal. Dredge well in flour, and brown in a skillet. Transfer the meatballs into a casserole.

Brown the onions and add them to the meatballs. Cover with equal amounts of beer and water. Add the nutmeg and vinegar and season to taste. Cook 20 minutes.

Recipe from In't Spinnekopke Restaurant in Brussels

Other Category
Belgian Coffee

In short, replace Irish whiskey with Chimay Bleue. Use a graduated Irish Coffee glass. Warm the trappist beer, without boiling. Add, according to your taste, a heaping tablespoon of brown sugar and a hint of cinnamon.

Pour this mixture into very strong, hot coffee, according to the measures on the glass. Pour the Chimay mixture gently. Never use instant coffee.

Delicately add single cream, pouring it in over a spoon.

Recipe available on the Chimay Brewery web site, and notably served at the Vaudrée I and II in Liège and Angleur.

1500 - 2000
500th anniversary of Charles Quint's birth.
A great monarch…and a great beer lover!

BEERS A TO Z

DESCRIPTION
AND
TASTING NOTES

A.D.A. Blonde des Pères
Top fermentation – Abbey
light blond
Brasserie du Val de Sambre, Gozée (Hainaut)
% 7

Tasting notes
This is a coppery blond, slightly cloudy. The head is abundant, pearly, and holds well. The nose develops accents of fruit and malt. Round and full in the mouth, it is hoppy and sweet. It leaves a pleasant bitterness, prolonged and well balanced.
terrine, veal liver

A.D.A5. Superbe
Top fermentation – Abbey
reddish brown

Brasserie du Val de Sambre, Gozée (Hainaut)
% 10

A.D.A. Triple
Top fermentation – Abbey
dark blond
Brasserie du Val de Sambre, Gozée (Hainaut)
% 9

Pub secret
In 1998, the beer from the Abbaye d'Aulne gained the enviable title of Médaille d'Or (Gold Medal) at the Hainaut championships.

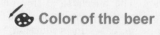 Color of the beer   % Percentage of alcohol

 Brewery   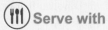 Serve with

Abbaye d'Aulne *(s. brewery p.135)*

In the VIIth century, Maurosus, a highway bandit, reappeared, travelling across the lands of his misdeeds in the hopes of seeing his injuries re-paid. He had converted to Catholicism, and he founded a first monastery, at Lobbes, in the valley of the Sambre. In keeping with his mission of evangelism, Maurosus spread himself around a little, and established a second abbey. He named it Aulne to evoke the trees that proliferated in the vicinity. The one time destroyer of rich travellers took as a baptism name Landelin, patron-name of the neighbouring village, Landelies, from the same root. In 1147 the religious community, attached to the principality of Liège by the Bishop Notger in 961, submitted to the rule of the Cistercians. Owing to its geographically critical position, Aulne become a required meeting ground of all warring parties. No doubt this is why, in 1794, the French revolutionaries didn't want to miss-out on their chance for any reason. Thanks to them, the Abbey at Aulne became the largest site of gothic ruins in the country, a rank it still holds today. Of course, the monks of the day included brewing beer in their activities. They probably brewed two of them, one light and one strong – these two recipes still being used in our day – with the production being of course interrupted along with the prayers.

A.D.A., as it is called, was resuscitated in 1904 and was, for a time, brewed in Dinant, before being transferred to the Bavery brewery in Couillet. Next it went to Opwijk, where it was produced by the Desmedt brewery, before landing finally in Saint-Amand, France. But, thanks to the perseverance of Jacques Wauthy, who is also vice-president of the Office of Walloon Products, the gamut of A.D.A. beers has been reintegrated into its original home. The ancient stables of the abbey have been fitted out as a small brewery, even so, with a total capacity of 15.000 litres. Even better, this move was part of a vast tourism project that integrates visits to the brewery, the ruins and of course, tasting local products. There is nothing left but to wait for the plan to come to fruition, but the plan alone is encouraging for the very deserving region.

Abbaye des Rocs *(s. brewery p.121)*

The Rocs brewery began in 1979 in fits and starts. In the beginning, the production totalled 50 litres every two weeks, produced after work hours in the Eloir family home. Thanks to help, most notably from two Trappist monks from Chimay, the recipe was improved little by little, and in 1987, a new building welcomed some 1500 litre vats. One of these had a long journey since it arrived from the old brewery Marbaix-la-Tour (Saison Régal) by way of Momignies (Chimay) and a brewery in the Mons region. The purchase of this new equipment permitted significant increases in production, so that in 1994 it reached 600 hectolitres per year. Two years later, another transformation and annual production passed 1000 hectolitres.

But in the mean time, help was waiting in the wings : after watching her parents brew for pleasure, Nathalie, now 31 years old, jumped into the game and decided to take up formal brewing studies. She became an engineering brewer and, to hear her mother tell it, the purist of the family : nothing escapes her attention as she works in collaboration with the laboratories at Louvin-la-Neuve. Today, the production capacity is 50 hl per vat and 3.000 hl annually.

Among the products of the brewery, we must point out the Abbaye des Rocs, a double density brown ale with a strong character and the Montagnarde, a triple density that can rival the most famous Trappist products. They have a common characteristic of being totally natural with no sugar or any other additives. Nathalie Eloir is also working on a beer based on fresh blackcurrant.

Abbaye des Rocs

Top fermentation – Abbey

🍺 brown - ruby

🍺 Brasserie de l'Abbaye des Rocs, Montignies sur Roc (Hainaut)

% 9

Tasting notes

This is a brown with red reflections, topped with an abundant, long-lasting head and a good release of gasses. In the nose, the scents of red fruits, a certain sweetness, malt and a presence of hops follow one another. In the mouth, it is acidic, heady, suggesting roasting, anis, liquorice, and hops. It capitalises on a fine, pronounced and prolonged bitterness.

🍴 veal kidneys

Achel

Top fermentation – Trappist

The monastery of Achel was founded in 1854, in a location not far from the border of Holland (the nearest town of any size being Eindhoven). Achel was the only Trappist abbey that did not produce beer, though brewing activity had existed up until the first World War. The Germans confiscated the copper of the vats, as they had in a series of other private breweries, and thus precipitated the disappearance of the Trappist beer from Achel. For more than 75 years, the monks would meet their financial needs by raising fruits and vegetables.

Perhaps because they tired of drinking the table beer of their neighbours from Westmalle every day, they recently decided to sell a part of their land, which they ceded for approximately 18 million BEF (445.000). The money permitted them an investment in a single brewing set-up and to begin their activities, under the benevolent eye of two consultants; one monk from Westmalle and one from Orval. And so, in the buildings that once served as the cowshed, they fitted out a café, the only place where one can today taste the newest holy brew.

Pub secret

Behind the scenes, it is said that the master brewer of Achel is a defector from the abbey of Westmalle, moreover, in agreement with neither his superiors in the hierarchy, nor the strict observance of rules extolled by the Cistercians. This is information that must be conditioned, since there is no proof either way, no smoke, no fire, but still...

Affligem *(s. brewery p.126)*

The beers of Affligem (near Hekelgem in Flemish Brabant) are not Trappists, even though they have all the qualities, and there still exists a monastic community at the abbey of the same name. So why not then? Simply because they are no longer brewed at that site, for the last 50 years, and in any event, the monks, re-installed next to the ruins of the ancient monastery – originally founded in 1083 – since 1870, follow the order of Saint Benoît (Benedictines), while Trappists are Cistercian. In short, a lot of confusion, but these are so close to legitimate that their brewing is confided only to specialists of the genre. As with most Trappists, the beer from Affligem is offered in several varieties.

Affligem Blond

Top fermentation – Abbey
🍺 light blond
📷 Brouwerij De Smedt, Opwijk (Flemish Brabant)
% 7

Tasting notes

This beer, brewed since 1950 by the monks of the abbey, develops a fine white foam, an average head and presents a golden blond body. It is a highly malted beer, revealing notes of citrus, a balanced acidity and a bitterness without excess.

🍽 meat balls in tomato sauce

Affligem Dubbel

Top fermentation – Abbey
🍺 translucent brown
📷 Brouwerij De Smedt, Opwijk (Flemish Brabant)
% 7

Tasting notes

This is a clear brown beer, with a good release of gasses and a light foam. Winy in the nose, it has a soft barley aroma. Very full in the mouth, it develops complex fruity flavours, a wine-like beginning, suggesting a note of passion fruit as well as light roasting flavours. A recognizable light bitterness, balanced and long lived.

🍽 saddle of hare, venison.

Affligem Tripel

Top fermentation – Abbey
🍺 dark blond
📷 Brouwerij De Smedt, Opwijk (Flemish Brabant)
% 8,5

Tasting notes

A clear blond with a persistent head, Affligem Triple has a fusty nose. The aroma is also fruity with notes of peach, smoke and caramel. Light when first tasted, it evolves into a strong finish in the mouth. It is a rich beer, acidic, soft and slightly bitter.

Pub secret

Abandoned by its founders after the Second World War, and ceded to the neighbouring brewery in Opwijk, Affligem is based on an *Antiqua Renovata Formula* which means "Renewed Ancient Formula". And as with *Port-Salut*, it says so on the bottom...

Augustijn *(s. brewery p.137)*

This authentic and classic abbey ale traces its history back to the Augustijner Abbey in Gent, founded in 1295. The abbey was a leading political, cultural and religious power house until well into the 17th century. As with all abbeys, their power and significance was broken by the French Revolution. It is in the 1950's that the Van Steenberge brewery started brewing the Augustijn beer under licence from the Abbey. The influx of new monks in the abbey dried up after WW II. The delicious Augustijn Abbey ales stand out among the many Belgian abbey ales.

The Augustijn Grand Cru, a true connoisseur's beer, will find many converts when served at room temperature. But the "truest of true" will appreciate it even more when served slightly cooler (in the neighbourhood of 8-9°C).

Augustijn

Top fermentation – Abbey

🍺 amber

🏭 Brouwerij Van Steenberge, Gent (East Flanders)

% 8

Tasting notes

Augustijn is a coppery blond, slightly cloudy. Its head is compact with only a weak release of gasses. It has aromas of barley and wheat, but it is also fruity and complex. Slightly piquant in the mouth, it develops a strong flavour of hops. The taste is characterised by a bitterness that is balanced and prolonged, finishing with herby and acidic notes.

Augustijn Grand Cru

Top fermentation – Abbey

🍺 amber

🏭 Brouwerij Van Steenberge, Gent (East Flanders)

% 9

Tasting notes

Strong for its 9%, this dim blond develops an abundant head that holds well, and a healthy release of gasses. The herby, complex nose also reveals malt and hops, which can also be tasted on the tongue. It is a full beer, slightly piquant, with a nicely presented, pronounced and prolonged bitterness.

🍴 terrine, ham omelette.

Barbar *(s. brewery p.131)*

Barbar, what a bizarre name for a honey beer with a sweet flavour. With such an appellation, a misinformed consumer might expect a much more aggressive brew. Nonetheless, the Lefebvre brewery has made no mistake. One senses the honey, without the sugar levels being exaggerated. Barbar is what we generally call a "bonne bière", with body in spades. It there-

duction is of 21,000 hectolitres. With its great freshness and low proof, it is particularly appreciated in Japan.

Barbar
Top fermentation – Other

🍺 dim blond, slightly cloudy

🏭Brasserie Lefebvre, Quenast (Walloon Brabant)

% 8

Tasting notes
Nicknamed "Bière du Guerrier" (the Warrior's Reward), this beautiful amber beer, with copper highlights, develops a compact and tenacious head. The release of gasses is average and the nose is sweet, offering whiffs of honey, barley and hops. Round in the mouth, it is also sweet and distinguishes itself with a pronounced bitterness, complex with a grassy note. The Barbar is also available in brown beer from October to February.

fore became the second representative of the honey beer category, after the aptly named Bière des Ours (Bear's Beer). From its appearance in 1995, it was warmly accepted and six European countries decided immediately to import it : France, the Netherlands, Great Britain, Italy, Spain and Portugal. Non-pasteurised, it is drunk from a mat glass for the principle reason that it better preserves the beer's cool temperature.

The Lefebvre brewery also markets an apple beer, produced with a base of Blanche de Bruxelles (Brussels White Beer). It is called Newton (think about it...), and its total annual pro-

Bavik *(s. brewery p.122)*
The Bavik brewery has been on the Belgian brewing landscape since 1894, which puts it among the oldest continuing operations in Belgium. They have brewed there, for many years, a pilsner that has never entered into competition with the stars of the market. It is a unique beer and, in spite of its character, has a very limited distribution network.

The brewery, which takes its name from Bavikhove, near

Harelbeke, is still independent and is also present in the "specials" beer market, notably with its *Petrus* triumvirate and the beautiful Wittekerke wheat beer. It also markets waters and soft drinks under the name Bon-Val. The water, which also serves as an ingredient to the beers, comes from a depth of 200 metres underground.

Bavik Premium Pils

Bottom fermentation – Pilsner

🐝 blond

📷 Brouwerij Bavik, Bavikhove (West Flanders)

% 5,5

Pub secret

In May 1994, the "best buy" title in the beer category was awarded to Bavik by the famous consumer magazine *Test Achats*.

Belle-Vue *(s. brewery p.131)*

It's inevitable : if you think of Gueze or Kriek, the name Belle-Vue pops into mind. It's not that it is the standard or even best, these things being more subjective, but it is surely thanks to the Belle-Vue brewery that the spontaneously fermented category has expanded beyond its originating region. It is also this brew that corresponds best to the tastes of the average consumer, and this brew that has the highest production numbers. Of course, we see it being exported, sometimes under the name of *La Bécasse*. Its history began in 1913, when a certain Philémon Vanden Stock became "coupeur" (cutter). This means that he was charged with elaborating the Gueuze with several Lambics purchased from other producers. Some years later, in 1927, he purchased a café-brewery, the Belle-Vue, in Anderlecht and thereby gave a name to his Gueuze.

After the Second World War, it was thanks to the influence of his son, Constant Vanden Stock – equally famous in the world of football, as he was for years the president of the Anderlecht Sporting Club – that the brewery underwent a major development. This allowed the distribution of Gueuze and its derivatives, until then little known outside their home region. Today, Belle-Vue is a division of Interbrew and benefits from the common marketing strategies of the other products of the group. The Belle-Vue brewery produces two distinct lines : the widely distributed Lambics, lightly sweetened, and the "Sélections" (Selects), composed of the highest quality Lambics, having ripened in casks for a minimum of 24 months and aged for 6 months after being bottled.

Belle-Vue (Framboise)

Spontaneous fermentation – Raspberry

🐝 light red, pink

📷 Brasserie Belle-Vue, Molenbeek St-Jean (Bruxelles)

% 5,2

Tasting notes

This oak barrel ripened beer presents an amber-pink body, beautiful light head and a strong raspberry nose. In the mouth, the coming together of the fresh Lambic and the subtle raspberry is ideal. It ends on notes of pear and banana and finishes crisply.

(⑪) terrine of game, pressed head-meat, raspberry Bavarian

Belle-Vue (Geuze)

Spontaneous fermentation – Gueuze

(🍺) amber, red-brown

(🏭) Brasserie Belle-Vue, Molenbeek St-Jean (Bruxelles)

% 5,2

Tasting notes

The abundant and tenacious foam tops a beer with a coppery blond body and a generous head. In the nose, it releases aromas of Lambic that are repeated in the mouth, balanced by an acidity and soft nuances, both bitter and smooth.

(⑪) cream cheese sandwich, croque-monsieur, herbed cheese

Belle-Vue (Kriek)

Spontaneous fermentation – Kriek (Cherry)

(🍺) ruby

(🏭) Brasserie Belle-Vue, Molenbeek St-Jean (Bruxelles)

% 5,2

Tasting notes

Belle-Vue Kriek has a beautiful ruby colour, a short-lived head and an average release of gasses. To the nose, it releases an aroma of Lambic, and very faint cherry. Piquant in the mouth, it is fairly acidic. Its flavour, identical to its aroma, is well presented and balanced, without bitterness.

Pub secret

Each year, the springtime salutes the return of the "Kriek Primeur". Brewed in July with young Lambic and the first cherries of the summer, it ripens eight months in the barrel before being cut with the new Lambic.

It is available beginning in the month of April.

Bière des Ours

Top fermentation – Other

(🍺) cloudy blond

(🏭) Brasserie La Binchoise, Binche (Hainaut)

% 8,5

Tasting notes

The "Bière des Ours" (Bear's Beer) presents a beautiful golden blond body, healthy gas release and a sturdy head of white foam. In the nose, one notes mostly barley, wheat and fine hops, while in the mouth it is very round, full, a little piquant and has a surprising note of hops. The flavour is herby, with passing notes of liquorice, anis and the sweetness due to the honey omnipresent.

(⑪) chicken waterzooi, blanquette of veal

Pub secret

The ramparts of Binche give proof, if any is needed, of the desire of the Binchoise to be present 365 days a year on the tourism scene. The fortifications were built by Baudouin IV, Count of Hainaut, around 1147. The bourgeoisie decided to enlarge the original in the first half of the XIIIth century. These then measured 2126 metres, with 30 towers and were pierced by six gates. In the centre of it all were the vestiges of the palace of Marie of Hungary, recalling the royal history of the city.

Blanche de Bruges (s. brewery p.126)

Just at the end of the XIXth century, the "Venice of the North" counted 31 breweries. "De Gouden Boom" (The Golden Tree) was one of these. Here was found, dating back to the XVth century, an inn known by the name of "'t Hamerken" which next became a distillery.

In 1872, Jules Vanneste purchased the facility and turned it into a brewery, to which he added a malting house three years later. You can still see the chimney in the buildings that today house the museum. The establishment was long one of the biggest breweries in the city, before its decline and end of production in 1976.

Six years later, the business was taken over by the Haacht brewery (Brabant), just a few months before operations took off again under the direction of Paul Vanneste, who was surely infected with the brewing bug by his ancestors. La Blanche (White Beer), which was the first of the "new" beers, has today entered under the direction of the Alken-Maes group. Like most of its contemporaries, its primary quality is its thirst quenching nature.

Blanche de Bruges Tarwebier

Top fermentation – White
🍺 lemon yellow, cloudy
🏭   Brouwerij "De Gouden Boom", Brugge (West Flanders)
% 4,8

Tasting notes

A straw yellow, cloudy beer, its head is white, abundant, dense and persistent. Slightly piquant, it offers a nose of young wheat and hops as well as notes of fruit and herbs. It has a weak bitterness, except in the finish. The

release of gasses is well balanced.

Pub secret

In 1998, the "De Gouden Boom" brewery received the "Trophée de la Haute Qualité Internationale" (International Trophy for High Quality) rewarding three successive gold medals at the Budapest championships.

Blanche de Haecht *(s. brewery p.129)*

Born in 1989, Blanche de Haecht is, in terms of production, the true understudy to the "queen" from Hoegaarden. Presented with much less fanfare than its competitor from Brabant, it takes up the old spelling of the region, as it was written in 1898, the year the brewery was created. The sower, allusion to the beer's richness in cereals, represented on the glass as well as the label, also dates from the same period.

Blanche de Haecht (Haecht Wit Bier)

Top fermentation – White
🍺 straw yellow
🏭   Brouwerij   Haacht, Boortmeerbeek   (Flemish Brabant)
% 4,7

Pub secret

Aside from the production of several beers, the Haacht brewery, like a few of its competitors, markets waters and soft drinks under the brand Val. What is less widely known is that Haacht has also had a wine department since 1960. It is essentially devoted to table wines and dinner wines. But the family has grown since 1995, since then the brewery has been the owner of a 12 ha vineyard, distributing under the appellations "Montagne St Emilion" and "St Georges St Emilion".

Since 1985, Haacht has held exclusive control of the commercial and industrial activities of Pepsi-Cola in Belgium.

Blanche de Hoegaarden (s. brewery p.131)

This is, without a doubt, the most famous Belgian white beer, in Belgium and abroad. Under the umbrella of Interbrew, it benefits from an uncommon amount of media publicity, like most of the groups other products. Outside of the traditional publicity outlets, Hoegaarden is also known by the angle of its infamous hexagonal coasters (like its glasses) with their often irreverent humour, and outside Belgium by the intermediary of the "Hoegaarden Cafés", symbolising a certain way of life. But, all this aside, Hoegaarden is probably one of the most appreciated of white beers because it is the most "approachable" in taste : neither too sweet nor too bitter with just enough spice and orange to make it a "modern" white beer, and one of today's stars of Belgium.

Blanche de Hoegaarden

Top fermentation – White
🍺 pale yellow, cloudy
🏭 Brouwerij De Kluis, Hoegaarden (Flemish Brabant)
% 5

Tasting notes

A slightly yellow wheat beer, Hoegaarden presents itself in a cloud of yeast, with a collar of bright foam and aromas of spiced fruits with a dominance of coriander and cool orange. Light and sweet, it must be served without a slice of citrus (which breaks the head and the taste).

🍴 Poached fish in cream sauce ; pastry

Pub secret

The first brewing of the "new" Hoegaarden by P. Célis was accomplished in a wooden barrel used for wine, with a volume of 600 litres. Cut into halves, the first half was used as a fermentation vat and the second as a proper brewing vat. The beer passed between in conduits made of wood. Today, the annual production reaches 900.000 hectolitres...

Blanche de Namur (s. brewery p.123)

It is said those from Namur are slow... but this reputation is sometimes completely unjustifiable. Want proof? Blanche de Namur was born in 1990, that is just two years after the advent of the one that touched off the white beer phenomenon. But, it wasn't happy just to be among the precursors : it also distinguishes itself by appearing different in body than what we normally associate with white beers. Lightly reddish brown, more bitter than average, it uses hard (red) wheat among the other cereals necessary to its brewing.

Blanche de Namur

Top fermentation – White
🍺 light amber

🏭 Brasserie du Bocq, Purnode (Namur)
% 4,5

Tasting notes

A cloudy yellow, Blanche de Namur develops an abundant release of gasses. Under its fine and short-lived head, it offers a nose of wheat, hops, coriander and lemon. Its flavour is piquant, with identical characteristics, accompanied by a late bitterness and balance, as well as a finish with a sensation of orange rind.

Boon (s. brewery p.123)

To say that the history of the Boon brewery is chaotic is a little like picking the lock on an open door. It all started in 1680 in Lembeek, the village that originated Lambic. The Claes family moved there and bought a farm where they installed a brewery and distillery. And well they did, as they pre-dated an imperial ordinance of 1720 that imposed a consumption tax on wines and grain alcohols. On Christmas Eve, 1794, the occupying French banned the distillation of *geniever* and the brewing of beer. Most brewers took the high road to Brussels, but others continued clandestinely. So much so, and so well in fact, that brewing was again tolerated a few years later...

The brewery, sold in 1860 to Louis Paul, was re-baptised "Brasserie Saint-Roch". In 1889, for lack of an inheritor, Louis Paul resold it to Pierre Troch, not without some renovation. The son of the latter, René, was unable to survive the economic crisis that followed World War I and, in 1927, ceded the land at public sale to Jean De Vits. The Second World War brought the loss of the vats (the copper taken by the enemy) and the beer was subsequently brewed by a cooperative society in Brussels.

René De Vits (the son of Jean), also being without an heir, sold his brewery to Frank Boon in 1978. The reserves of Lambic needed to be replenished and the machinery modernised. In 1986, the brewery invested in new land and two years later, a brewing room, preceded by a steam brewing vat and bottling cellar. The Gueuze, or rather *Geuze,* was reborn in its native region. Today, the F. Boon brewery falls under Palm, though it retains its independence.

Boon (Framboise)

Spontaneous fermentation – Raspberry

🍇 intense red

🏭 Brouwerij Frank Boon, Lembeek (Flemish Brabant)
% 5

Tasting notes

The Framboise (Raspberry) presents a body of deep red, almost amber, with a bright head. It develops a strong aroma of young red wine, very fruity and a little woody. In the mouth there appears, under a pleasant acidity slightly tannic and full of Lambic, ripe cherry and raspberry flavours, with notes of young Bordeaux, vanilla, wood and lemon. It is served at 8°C.

🍴 as aperitif, with entree or salad with vinaigrette (raspberry vinegar)

Pub secret

In the years around 1875, Louis Paul, the owner at that time, made several attempts at bottling his Gueuze-Lambic. But the bottles exploded ! The cause : too much pressure or glass too thin, history doesn't tell us...

Boon (Geuze)

Spontaneous fermentation – Gueuze

🍺 coppery

📷 Brouwerij Frank Boon, Lembeek (Flemish Brabant)

% 6

Tasting notes

This mix of bottle re-fermented, young and old Lambics presents an abundant head, a floral aroma accompanied by notes of ginger, and a dry finish, woody and slightly salty. It is best tasted when served at 13°C.

Boon Mariage Parfait (Kriek)

Spontaneous fermentation – Kriek (Cherry)

🍺 amber – red

📷 Brouwerij Frank Boon, Lembeek (Flemish Brabant)

% 5

Tasting notes

A light brown colour, slightly reddish, this beer presents a bright foam and a winy, fruity, floral nose. Its Lambic nose is also slightly sulphurous and tart and delivers aromas of prune, cherry, nut, wood and cheese. One discovers exactly the same characteristics in the mouth where it also feels bitter and dry. It delivers a nice fruity flavour.

Bornem Double (s. brewery p.137)

Top fermentation - Abbey

🍺 dark

📷 Brouwerij Van Steenberge, Gent (East Flanders)

% 8

Tasting notes

Very dark, coffee color. Full rich body with a malty character, leaves a velvety feeling in the mouth, and a "hoppy" after-touch—very luscious.

Monks used to fast on this type of beer for 40 days! No food, only beer! This Bornem Double can compete and beat any Belgian Abbey or Trappist double, like it did in the 1995 California Microbrew festival. This beer offers great "food" value, and is ideal with steak, grilled meat, game or sausages. It is a power shot after physical exercises, and recommended to nursing mothers in Belgium. It is refermented in the bottle and in the keg.

Originally brewed by the St. Bernardus abbey in Bornem, near Antwerpen, it is now brewed under license by the Van Steenberge family brewery, using the original yeast and recipe. In the 1950's most abbeys ceased to brew their own beer, since the influx of new monks dried up.

Bornem Triple

Top fermentation - Abbey

🍺 pale

📷 Brouwerij Van Steenberge, Gent (East Flanders)

% 9

Tasting notes

Splendid aroma, a soft feeling in the mouth, perfectly balanced taste, tickling in the nose, with a "hoppy" dry finish. This classic Abbey triple, pale in color, outshines most other Abbey triples. This one is refermented in the bottle and in the keg! You can age this beer for many years. Triples used to be reserved for the Bishops and the Abbots. They knew what was good!

The abbey of Bornem traces its history back to 1237, when Cistercienzer monks started the abbey on the borders of the river Scheld near Antwerpen. It became an important religious, cultural and political center in the 'Low Lands'. The French Revolutionaries plundered and burned the abbey, and the monks had to flee. Later a new group of monks rebuilt the abbey a few miles further in Bornem. Br. Van Steenberge pays license fees to the abbey for the privilege to brew and sell their beer.

🍷 filet of duck with cherries, crème caramel

Bourgogne des Flandres *(s. brewery p.135)*

On the flats between Flanders and Bourgogne, history has often passed. To such a degree in fact that the two regions retain its traces. So, there is nothing surprising about a beer named Bourgogne des Flandres, especially with its reflection of the fruits of the vine, so ample nearby. To perfect the whole image, the belfry of Bruges stands proudly on the label, as if it were needed to remind us of the degree to which the city is anchored in history. Started by the Van Houtrijve brewery in the

first years of the XXth century, this beer is brewed today by Timmermans, itself controlled by the John Martin group.

Bourgogne des Flandres

Top fermentation – Flemish brown

🍺 dark brown

🏭 Brouwerij Timmermans, Itterbeek (Flemish Brabant)

% 5

Tasting notes

Under a creamy head, Bourgogne des Flandres, with a colour almost black, delivers a fresh acidity to the nose. It is a little flat in the mouth and its taste, short but strong, is characterised by roasting flavours and caramel.

🍷 fried fish and tartar sauce

Brigand *(s. brewery p.137)*

Here again is an appellation without a well defined origin: this beer takes its name from either the highway bandits that ravaged Flanders in the XVIIIth century, or the Flemish farmers, nicknamed "les Brigands", who helped deliver the region from the French enemy in 1798. Elsewhere they served in combat against the Sans-Culottes, also in the end of the XVIIIth century. We leave you to choose the history that pleases you most ! Outside of these concerns, Brigand first appeared on tables in 1980, thanks to the Van Honsebrouck family. It presents itself under a white and abundant head, and possesses an undeniable character. Its glass, with a marvellously worked foot, is in itself worth the trip. In 1999, its label underwent a slight *facelift*.

Brigand

Top fermentation – Other
🍺 amber
🏭 Brouwerij Van Honsebrouck, Ingelmunster (West Flanders)
% 9

Tasting notes

Brigand has a beautiful golden blond body and a lingering head. No release of gasses is noticed. In the nose, one senses above all aromas of fresh hops. Its characteristics are similar in the mouth, where it is slightly piquant. It finishes with a bitterness that is healthy and prolonged.

Pub secret

Shortly after its launch into export, Brigand made a true success, thanks to it promotion and the ideas of its papa, Luc Van Honsebrouck. The promotion centred on an "ambiance champagne" ("champagne lifestyle"). Packaged in 75cl, it was accompanied by a basket and was served in its familiar balloon glass. It was immediately popular.

Bruegel (s. brewery p.137)

Top fermentation - Other
🍺 amber
🏭 Brouwerij Van Steenberge, Gent (East Flanders)
% 5

Tasting notes

Bruegel is an easy drinking, soft and tasty amber ale. Thanks to the refermentation in the bottle and in the keg, it offers more body, more head and more taste than most other Belgian amber ales. It is brewed with Dutch barley and German hops. Although the bitterness is clearly present it is not overbearing at all, and becomes the ideal alternative for the common "hoppier" pilsner. Young people's taste buds are unfortunately corrupted by the sweetness of sodas, which make them appreciate sweeter beers. Bruegel goes with meat, salads and fish without any problem. It's a party beer because of its excellence.

Brugse Tripel (s. brewery p.126)

This is the other flower, alongside the "Blanche de Bruges", of the "De Gouden Boom" brewery. Michael David says of it that it is brewed with passion and aged with care. And it is true that this triple-dense benefits from all the attentions of its brewer, and that it is loaded with the qualities of the greats. Golden, like the "Boom" (Tree) at the foot of which it rests, it demands a notoriety equal to its qualities.

Brugse Tripel

Top fermentation – Other
🍺 amber – blond
🏭 Brouwerij De Gouden Boom, Brugge (West Flanders)
% 9

Tasting notes

An amber-blond beer, re-fermented in the bottle, it offers a nice, compact, creamy coloured head and a cloudy body. The fruity nose is accompanied by points of caramel and malt. The approach is a little piquant, powerful even, in the mouth. Joining it are roasting flavours,

Brasserie De Gouden Boom

a taste of honey and a prolonged bitterness. It is ideally served in its tall, footed glass, between 8 and 12°C.

Bush (called Scaldis in the USA)
(s. brewery p.127)

The oldest Walloon family brewery celebrated in 1999 its 230 years of existence, and remains very attached to its independence. Its origin goes back to 1769, when Joseph Leroy, then in the service of the master of the estate, decided to branch out and establish himself as an independent farmer-brewer. In 1931, agricultural activities were completely abandoned and two years later, Alfred and Amédée Dubuisson launched what would become one of the flowers of Belgian brewing culture, *Bush Beer*, which means simply "beer of the forest". Responding to a demand of the time, it strongly resembles English beers.

In our days, it is still, with its 12%, the most alcoholic Belgian beer. Over the years, it would take up a larger and larger popularity, to a point when in 1981 the production of other beers was halted. *Bush 12* wouldn't remain alone for long, because Noël Bush appeared in 1991. And three years later, on the occasion of the brewery's 225th anniversary, a third pretender made its appearance under the name *Bush 7* (in French vernacular pronounced "Bûchette" or "little Bush"). In 1999, on the occasion of the 65th anniversary (an age that does not signify retirement in this case) of the eldest in the family, the brewery welcomed a newcomer, *Bush Blonde* (10,5%). Note that at the same time, *Bush 12* was re-baptised as *Bush Ambrée* (Amber), and that its label underwent a beautiful facelift.

Rewarded with multiple awards from international competitions (since 1935 up to the recent Eurobière salon in 1999), Bush appears all over the world, from Canada to South Africa, by way

Color of the beer

Brewery

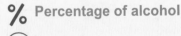
% **Percentage of alcohol**

Serve with

of Brazil, and Japan. Even so, it continues to take care of its hometown with 60% of its production being destined to the province of Hainaut alone.

Bush 7
Top fermentation – Other
🍺 light amber
🏭 Brasserie Dubuisson, Pipaix (Hainaut)
% 7,5

Tasting notes

"Bush 7" is a coppery, clear blond that offers a bubbly pour and generous head that holds well. One picks up notes of violet, hops, peppermint and coriander, while appreciating a pleasant, well-balanced bitterness.

Pub secret

A venerable "grandfather" of 230 years evidently has a lot of little stories to tell, and the most surprising is the one that follows. For the occasion of his entry into the White House, President George ... Bush was delivered, from the Dubuisson brewery, a small cargo of their bubbly product, marketed under the name of Scaldis in the United States. The elect of the American nation sent a communiqué saying "that he appreciated it". A humorous interlude and a publicity coup !!

Bush Ambrée
Top fermentation – Other
🍺 amber
🏭 Brasserie Dubuisson, Pipaix (Hainaut)
% 12

Tasting notes

The colour of "old gold", Bush presents abundant bubbles, a compact head and a nose of malted barley. It is a powerful beer, with a pronounced flavour of roasted malt, with notes of pear and caramel, prolonged by a pleasant bitterness.

Cantillon *(s. brewery p.124)*

We are in 2000, this year, and Cantillon is 100 years old. Its history begins with a probable misunderstanding in the family, which obliged Paul Cantillon to leave Lembeek, his birth-village, and install himself in Anderlecht, in the Cureghem quarter. The choice of location was in large part due to the oppressive taxes that were slapped on the businesses of Brussels proper. September 12, 1900 then saw the birth of the brewery in the same location where it exists today.

The two words that come most rapidly to mind when describing Jean-Pierre Van Roy are *family* and *natural*. Family because the spirited 100 year old has never changed hands, today's proprietor being the son-in-law of Marcel Cantillon. What's more, its sure to stay put as the children and grand children involve themselves more and more in the business. Natural because the production of beers without the use of any type of additive has always been ... natural among the Cantillons. The brewery, that is today the last craft brewery in Brussels, concentrates on beers free of "outside" influences and hopes to obtain the "Bio" classification in 2002. Besides its "classic" products, Cantillon makes a beer that is unique in the world : Iris. Spontaneously fermented, it is completely dif-

ferent from its neighbouring brews by the fact that it is produced without wheat (Lambic normally has about 35%). Aged two years in barrels and re-fermented in the bottle, it is also made with fresh hops, which gives it a particular bitterness. To make a little history, note that the iris is the official flower of Brussels and its region.

For more than 20 years, the brewery has organised regular public brewing days, allowing interested persons to taste and appreciate the different steps of production.

The Cantillon beers have recently been distributed by Delhaize Le Lion, which is the first chain of supermarkets to market them.

Caracole *(s. brewery p.124)*

"Yet another beer out of the lower Walloon region" say some smart alecks. This choice of words is in especially poor judgement, as they are said of a brew of excellent manufacture.

In the Namur area of the Walloon region, *Caracole* means *snail*, a sympathetic allusion to the supposed slowness of its inhabitants. The founders of the brewery, François Tonglet and Jean-Pierre Debras, originally from down there, decided one day in 1986 to put themselves to producing beer and set their sights on ... the centre of town. The trials and errors would take four years before the first beer, worthy of the name, appeared.

But very quickly, the space proved too small, and while searching out new locations and better suited materials, our compatriots learned that the Lamotte brewery, located in Falmignoul and closed since the early seventies, was for sale. By luck, there were repairable materials and, in 1992, the business took off again. It was the beginning of an adventure as much for the new owners, who wanted to cut the umbilical cord with their origins, as for the brewery. It already had a long history of its own : created in the XVIIIth century by a certain Moussoux family, it was taken over in the beginning of the thirties by the Lamotte family who held the reins for forty years. The purchase of this location had then a flavour of perpetuation.

The first brew was produced there in 1994. To the *Caracole ambrée* was quickly added a brown version, the *Cuvée 9°*, a *Saxo* – the brewery is situated very near Dinant, the birth-village of Adolphe Sax –, a white with the beautiful name *Troublette* ("cloudy" or "troubled" one) and finally a "Bio" evolution.

Since its launch, the brewery has become more "professional" without losing its craft character. The production increases have never waned and there are good omens for expansion. Its beers received beautiful new labels, in line with the popular habit of giving a more or less ecclesiastical air to regional beers. The Caracole brewery also welcomed within its doors a certain Charles Fontaine, a highly decorated and well-known figure in brewing circles. Head over heels about beer, he is noted for opening a museum dedicated to brewery vehicles and is at the heart of the resuscitation of Faro in Brussels. Rest assured that the little business in Dinant is in very good hands.

Caracole Ambrée

Top fermentation – Other

🍺 like the name says, amber

🏭 Brasserie Caracole, Falmignoul (Namur)

% 7,2

Tasting notes

Caracole Ambrée presents a hearty release of gasses and a compact head that holds well. To the nose, it offers aromas of hops and a few marine notes. It is slightly piquant in the mouth ; one senses hops, a light roasting and a pleasant, balanced and prolonged bitterness. It is also marked by points of orange blossom, mocha and liquorice.

Carolus d'Or *(s. brewery p.129)*

Gouden Carolus (Golden Carolus) returns to honour what is called a "grande bière". Made from the upper most results of the fermentation vats, it was destined for the rich and famous. It was, at Malines, the beer that one consumed during the big fox hunt. A Carolus D'or or *Gouden Carolus* was the name of a piece of furniture used in the time of Charles Quint, the emperor whose 500th anniversary we celebrate this year. Charles Quint was born in Gand, but was raised mainly in Malines – the Belgian village with the most registered monuments – by Margaret of Austria, his aunt, long-time governor of the Netherlands. Later, while he ruled Europe, the emperor had beer brought from the "Het Anker" brewery to his residence in Spain. Since the family also had ties to Bourgogne, it is only natural that this beer, which in a way pays tribute to the man with the empire on which the sun never set, has something in common with the vintages of Bourgogne.

It was also logical that the "Het Anker" (The Anchor) brewery, established in Malines since the XVth century, thanks to the generosity of Charles "le Téméraire" (the Brave), should decide to improve this traditional brew. In 1873 the brewery became the property of the Van Breedam family, who made of it a modern enterprise, using the "cutting edge" techniques of the time. After the Second World War, the brewery re-centred its activities, a little against the current, and devoted itself to the improvement of its special beers. Today, the only exception is the *Den Blusser*, a low fermented beer (Pilsner) that has been marketed since 1999. Strongly hopped, it releases a confident personality. On the other hand, like its brewery sisters, it evokes the history of Malines. *Maneblusser* is, in fact, the nickname of the Malines natives, and is translated as "extinguisher", according to the visions of a drunkard who believed that a fire had broken out at the Tour St Rombaut.

Recently, *Gouden Carolus* undertook a facelift for its label. We still see Charles Quint there, represented with a simple face, but dressed by the draftsman in an ensemble entirely of black and gold, thereby reinforcing the "royal" character.

Each year, the 24th of February, a slightly modified version, called Cuvée de l'Empereur or Cuvee van de Keizer is brewed in limited quantities for the occasion of Charles Quint's birthday. It's not a proper seasonal or "special event" beer like one normally finds. In this case, we are instead in the presence of a veritable "vintage beer". In fact, the brewer explains that the date chosen is really just a pretext for producing a completely unique brew. The object in mind is to produce a beer of the same philosophy as great wines : one sole annual production and, therefore, an absolutely uniform quality of production.

Cuvée de l'Empereur isn't really available outside of the brewery (90% of the production) and can be stored without worry for 10 years in the cellar.

Carolus d'Or

Top fermentation – Other

🍷 reddish brown

🏭 Brouwerij Het Anker, Mechelen (Anvers)

% 7,5

Tasting notes

Gouden Carolus offers a beautiful dark brown body with red highlights, a creamy and persistent head, and a good release of gasses. It comes with a nose of powerful scents, underlined by notes of banana, port and cherry. In the mouth, it develops a rich, malted bitterness, imprinted with sweetness and flavours of banana and caramel.

🍴 game, wild mushrooms, herbed bread

Chapeau ("Hat") *(s. brewery p.126)*

The De Troch brewery, is their head too big for their hat ? Of course not, in person they are a completely normal family and there's nothing to worry about. Though it must be said that they are originals ! To that point, in addition to their classic products like their Gueuze, Kriek, Faro and raspberry beer, one finds a collection of seven beers infused with diverse aromas (in order : apricot, banana, citrus, exotic, peach, plum and strawberry). There you see what instilled revolution in the relatively conservative world of spontaneously fermented beers. But Jos Raes, the father of these "specialties", put his cards on the table when he announced : it is the aromas that define the flavour of each of these modern beers. So, no worms in the fruit then, but

Brasserie DE TROCH BVBA   LANGESTRAAT 20   1741 TERNAT-WAMBEEK
TEL 02/582 10 27   FAX 02/582 72 41   E-MAIL detroch@unicall.be

surely fruit-beer in the glass. ("*Pas de ver dans le fruit donc, mais du fruité dans le verre, assurément.*") Truly, it had to be done, so to him, we tip our ... hat!

But the De Troch brewery isn't in its infancy. A survey map proves this, because there we find continual signs of this brewery back to the beginning of the XIXth century. The brewer of that time was a woman, a certain Petronella De Troch. There was however beer brewed at Wambeek before this because we know that the father of Petronella brewed it before her. The rest of the story is that the little family enterprise remains one of the oldest in its region, and is fiercely attached to its independence.

Chapeau Banana

Spontaneous fermentation – Gueuze

🍺 lightly golden

🏭 Brouwerij De Troch, Wambeek (Flemish Brabant)

% 3

Tasting notes

On a visual level, one notes essentially a clear Pilsner colour and a white, short-lived head. The nose discerns an artificial aroma of banana as well as peach and malt in the background. In the mouth, the acid and sweet taste is quickly replaced by an artificial banana flavour.

🍴 bananas flambé

Chapeau Exotic

Spontaneous fermentation – Gueuze

🍺 golden, almost opaque

🏭 Brouwerij De Troch, Wambeek (Flemish Brabant)

% 3

Tasting notes

Like the "Chapeau Banana", one sees a Pilsner coloured body and a light head. The principle characteristics that rise to the nose are scents of pineapple, malt and butter. In the mouth, its approach is acidic and sugary with an artificial pineapple flavour. It finishes sweeter.

🍴 Hawaiian pizza, exotic salad

The Legend of Charles Quint

The exact location where the following story took place is not known, and this gives rise to variants that place it in either Flanders or the Walloon region. Here is the version told in the region of Walcourt. "Charles Quint, whose 500th anniversary we celebrate this year, entered a tavern one fine day and ordered a beer. The pub keeper poured it and offered it in a mug, holding it by the handle. The emperor refused it, under the pretext that he could not seize it properly. A little while later, again in the region, the little game started again. But this time, the pub keeper presented him a mug with two handles, which Charles Quint refused because the owner gripped it with both hands. The third try was met again with rejection. The pub keeper didn't think to offer the mug with the third handle pointed towards the emperor. A fourth try was needed, and so there are four handles on the mug, so Charles Quint can drink to his heart's content."

Chapeau Fraise

Spontaneous fermentation – Gueuze

🍷 red orange

🏭 Brouwerij De Troch, Wambeek (Flemish Brabant)

% 3

Tasting notes

Its brown cloudy body is topped with a reddish brown head. The artificial strawberry odour calls to mind yoghurt or candy. There is a noticeable lack of beer aroma. In the mouth there is a remarkable mix of acidity and sweetness, a hint of bitterness and a strong perfume of artificial strawberry flavour. A lightly bitter aftertaste defines the finish.

🍴 strawberry desserts

Charles Quint *(s. brewery p.129)*

In the year of grace 1500, a prince named Charles was born in Gand. Less than twenty years later, he was to be proclaimed Emperor of Germany and thereby reign over a large part of the world. This jubilee year is therefore an excellent occasion for the Haacht brewery to spruce up this beer launched in 1978. The packaging has been re-examined and the brewing has been improved. A good way to honour one of the greatest heads of state in history, of whom it is said he much preferred beer to wine, a phenomenon sadly rare in our time.

To better appreciate it, in addition to the "classic" chalice glass which reveals its beautiful coppery red colour, there is the legendary jug with four (or three) handles that recalls yesteryear, while true amateurs won't lack appreciation for it as an ingredient in many recipes concocted by some of our great master chefs.

Charles Quint
Top fermentation – Other
🦀 coppery red
📷 Brouwerij Haacht, Boortmeerbeek (Flemish Brabant)
% 9

Tasting notes
This is a dark brown beer, made using top fermentation, lightly fruity, soft and sweet. Its foam is abundant and holds well and it presents an abundant head. In the nose there is, above all else, malt, accompanied by notes of Port. In the mouth it is acidic but presents a pleasant, prolonged, balanced bitterness. There are also notable traces of roasting, liquorice and a pronounced mocha flavour.

Pub secret
Be aware that this anniversary year, already kicked-off in October 1999 in Gand, has been and will continue to be an occasion for festivals and parties in many Belgian villages, marked by a visit from the Emperor.

Cherish Lambic (s. brewery p.137)
Spontaneous fermentation – Other
🦀 fruit lambic
📷 Brouwerij Van Steenberge, Gent (East Flanders)
% 5

Tasting notes
This very pleasant Lambic comes in three flavors: Cherry, Peach and Raspberry—the Cherry being more popular in Europe, the Raspberry being the most popular one in the USA. All three have the dominant flavor of the fruit, with its natural sweetness, but still the taste of Lambic, which is sour by nature. This Lambic stands out of the pack, because of a light bitterness of hops in the aftertaste. It amazingly enforces the taste of the fruit.. The Cherish is not as sweet as most popular Lambics, which have changed over time to accommodate the sweet cravings of young consumers.

Cherish fruit beers are in high demand at celebrations and parties where they replace Champagne, and other sparkling wines—they are so much better! You can also enjoy it just for "fun in the sun." Drink a peach with a very spicy curry dish, a raspberry with a fruit cake or even a chocolate cake. Drink the cherry as a first class thirst quencher.

Chimay (s. brewery p.124)
January 13th 2000 the "Bières de Chimay" brewery received from the hand of Prince Philippe, the *Royal Export Award*. Truly, this was a great commendation for this enterprise that conducts more than 34% of its business outside of Belgium and whose foreign growth was equal to almost 50% of the total growth of C.A. for the period 1990-1999.

Its history started in 1850. The prince of Chimay at the time had a particularly good idea : offer a part of his lands to a new monastic order. Thanks to this act, seventeen monks from Westvleteren (it is said that if they knew at the beginning what they were in for ...) were able to begin the construction of an abbey according to Cistercian rules and, beginning in 1862, brew their own beer. They worked with a soft water – bubbling into their basement and needing no adjustment in its ph – and offered to Belgium its fifth Trappist beer. But in our day, though the brewing, which tops 100.000 hectolitres per year, continues to take place within the abbey walls, *sine qua non* condition for the "Trappist" title, the racking and bottling have been confided, since 1978, to the lay community so as not to interrupt the community's work in meditation. These two operations take place in Baileux and the site hums to a rhythm of 35.000 bottles per hour.

But, coming back to the numbers : the entire production represents 13% of the market for specialty beers in Belgium and in 1999, the exports were close to 30.000 hectolitres. As for impact on the environment, they seem to be under control since the brewery was endowed with a water purification plant in 1996 and the quantity of packaging lost is less than 1%. The future seems to be secure then for the brewery and the 67 people it employs.

Finally, we would be remiss if we did not include a gentle remembrance of Frère Thomas, the emblematic and debonair master-brewer, deceased during the writing of this guide ...

Chimay Bleue or Grande Réserve

Top fermentation – Trappist

🍺 brown

🍺 Bières de Chimay, Chimay (Hainaut)

% 9

Tasting notes

Chimay Bleue – the only one to be date stamped – presents itself in dark fullness with a fruity aroma. It shows a beautiful brown body and brown head, abundant and tenacious. It releases an abundant amount of gasses and has a fruity nose. Its taste is piquant, with a long bitterness and a pronounced roasting flavour.

Chimay Rouge or Chimay Première

Top fermentation – Trappist

🍺 amber

🍺 Bières de Chimay, Chimay (Hainaut)

% 7

Tasting notes

It characterises itself with a light coppery-brown colour and a very smooth taste. Best served between 10 and 12°C, it develops a head that holds well. Its has a significant softness in the nose and carries notes of hops and roasted barley. In the mouth, it is slightly piquant in spite of its overall softness. One notices a balanced bitterness and a touch of vanilla.

Chimay Triple or Cinq Cents

Top fermentation – Trappist

🍺 amber

🍺 Bières de Chimay, Chimay (Hainaut)

% 8

Tasting notes

Triple gilt with a refreshing bitterness, it is best tasted between 6 and 8°C . Its coppery blond colour and abundant gas release is topped with a beautiful and generous head, creamy and compact. It offers a nose of hops and wheat. In the mouth it is full and leaves a prolonged bitterness. Its taste presents notes of anis and nuances of herbs while the aftertaste leaves a milky impression.

Pub secret

Recently called Chimay Blanche, this last beer was re-baptised Chimay Triple in order to avoid any confusion with products of another type ... the Abbaye de Scourmont not being united with Hoegaarden, far from it ...

Chouffe *(s. brewery p.121)*

Its history began in 1982 and is told during the long winter evenings of the region, a little like a legend of the Ardennes. Two brothers-in-law, one Walloon and one Flemish, made beer brewing their passion. They produced four micro-batches of 49 litres before giving it a name, Chouffe, inspired by the village (Achouffe) and the local vernacular in which a *chouffe* is a small imp, also called a *nutton*, found only in the local tales. In 1987, McChouffe set its sites on its predecessor, and was quickly nicknamed "the Scotch of the Ardennes". The fairy tale ends here to make room for a much more serious enterprise : the opening of export operations (66% of its production), new advanced facilities, a growing pres-

ence manifested in many ways, production in excess of 13000 hectolitres annually, relocation of the bottling operations to larger facilities,... In brief, the little family brewery appears to be securely on the rails to success.

Chouffe is accompanied by its cheese, *Patachouffe*, well matched to the beer.

Chouffe

Top fermentation – Other

🍺 amber

📷 Brasserie d'Achouffe, Achouffe (Luxembourg)

% 8

Tasting notes

We find ourselves in the presence of a coppery blond beer, slightly cloudy, offering a nice head of foam, white and compact. There is a significant amount of gasses released. To the nose, it is fairly complex, with hints of barley, wheat and hops, with an herby background. Very round and full in the mouth, it reveals a pleasant, balanced bitterness, a fruity complexity and a note of raspberry.

(🍴) Lamb chops.

Ciney *(s. brewery p.122)*

A little revolution in the constantly changing world of Belgian brewers : the Alken-Maes brewery, who has brewed Ciney under license for sometime already, just (in February 2000) acquired the ownership rights of the brand. So therefore, the familiar product of the old Demarche brewery falls one hundred percent under the umbrella of Europe's number two brewing group. In practice, this certainly means the playing field for this trilogy from Condroz will likely expand considerably. Something that is merited by these three beers, of which the common characteristic is a classic sweet-bitterness.

Often ranked as an abbey beer, this beer has nothing ecclesiastical about it. The belfry on the label is simply the belfry of the church in the little town of Condroz. And it is not, then, from the orthodox monastery, nearby, of Chevetogne which might have given the beer a slightly pious feel.

Ciney Blonde

Top fermentation – Other
🍺 blond
🏭 Brasserie de l'Union, Jumet (Hainaut)
% 7

Tasting notes

Ciney Blonde is resplendent thanks to its beautiful golden blond colour. It gives only a light release of gasses but develops a good head, abundant and tenacious. In its characteristic glass, a nose of barley and fresh hops is uncovered. A little piquant in the mouth, it delivers powerful malt, underlined by flavours of hops, caramel and a light roasting taste. In its finish, it reveals a balanced and prolonged bitterness.
(🍽) hard rind cheese, roasted chicken

Ciney Brune

Top fermentation – Other
🍺 ochre brown
🏭 Brasserie de l'Union, Jumet (Hainaut)
% 7

Tasting notes

Ciney Brune has red highlights, an abundant and tenacious head and an average release of gasses. To the nose, it is fairly soft and reveals a light roasting accompanied by aromas of malt and liquorice. In the mouth, it is soft, sweet, round, presents a light roasting flavour and a balanced bitterness with notes of banana.
(🍽) wild boar stew

Ciney Spéciale

Top fermentation – Other
🍺 brown
🏭 Brasserie de l'Union, Jumet (Hainaut)
% 9

Tasting notes

Ciney Spéciale reveals a strong brown body and a significant release of gasses under a beautiful creamy head that holds well. Its nose is distinguished by fruit and roasting aromas. In the mouth, it is piquant, full and round. Roasting flavours reappear, to which are added flavours of banana, mocha and liquorice.

Pub secret

Evolution or revolution? It's a question worth asking. Today, and since the end of 1999, Ciney Blonde is available in 50cl metal cans. Bizarre, huh ? What's next, Trappists in vending machines ... !!?

Corsendonk

Top fermentation – Abbey
Here's an example of a "Belgian Compromise" : there are two Corsendonks, one brewed in Flanders and one brewed in the Walloon region... and it's a

third brewery that distributes them ! Seriously though, this beer takes its name from the abbey of the same name, founded in the XIVth century in De Kempen. There they brewed a beer, whose production was halted because of... the French Revolution. At the beginning of our century, a brewer from Turnhout took the recipe out of storage and marketed a "Patersbier" with similar characteristics to the real Corsendonk Pater. But it is only over a period of twenty years that the beer has really taken off, thanks in part to its packaging being redesigned in a more pleasing manner, (a serigraph of a monastic decoration on the bottle).

From a more pragmatic point of view, the two Corsendonks are very different, with the advantage of smoothness going to the brown. This one also benefits from a longer resting period : about 20 days at 22°C.

Corsendonk Agnus (s. brewery p.123)

🍺 pale blond
🏭 Brasserie du Bocq, Purnode (Namur)
% 8

Tasting notes

A refined blond of Top fermentation, Agnus develops a persistent head. It releases a perfume of hops that pleases the nose, spicy, with aromas of fruit and crème fraîche. Soft in the mouth, it is also spicy and possesses a pleasant prolonged bitterness.

Corsendonk Pater (s. brewery p.137)

🍺 rusty brown

🏭 Brouwerij Van Steenberge, Ertvelde (East Flanders)
% 8

Tasting notes

The "Pater" is a brown with a fruity bouquet and a flavour of malt. Relatively sweet, the finish is also malty. It is best served between 8 and 10°C.

Cuvée de l'Ermitage (s. brewery p.122)

Cuvée de L'Ermitage (taking its name from the hermitage at Cocar, near Dour) is the pride of the Union brewery, of which it is a pure product since it was brewed before the unification with Alken. The Cuvée has been available for tasting since the 50s, when its creator realised his dream of at least fifteen years. The recipe, though not associated with monks, nonetheless came from the ancient products of hermits living in autarky. It makes an impression with the quality and tenacity of its head, as well as the immense size of its glass. With its perfect roundness, it invites only the learned and confident beer taster. The Cuvée de l'Ermitage has won multiple medals at various international competitions.

Cuvée de l'Ermitage

Top fermentation – Abbey
🍺 dark amber
🏭 Brasserie de l'Union, Jumet (Hainaut)
% 8

Tasting notes

The Cuvée de l'Ermitage has an amber body and barely discernable aromas of fruit. It is a sly beer, that finishes with

flavours of coconut and chocolate. It is also lightly hoppy.

Cuvee van de Keizer

Top fermentation – Other

🎨 dark brown

🏭 Brouwerij Het Anker, Mechelen (Anvers)

% 8,5

Pub secret

Unique in Belgium, the Het Anker brewery opened, in August 1999, a small hotel-restaurant with 22 rooms in the heart of an ancient storehouse. One can taste there a range of cuisine based mostly on beer. It is an original and amusing way to discover the region, in keeping with the purpose of the brewery that wishes to attract people inside its walls rather than open itself out to the exterior (cafés, stores ...).

De Koninck *(s. brewery p.126)*

Anvers (Antwerp) is the number two city in Belgium, the first city of Flanders and the third city in the world. The De Koninck brewery is the last Antwerpen brewery, in existence since 1833 under different appellations and has been directed since 1919 by the Van den Boogaert family. The stage is set, and these are the conditions under which De Koninck (an amusing aside is that it has no given name, only a family name) is and remains the favourite beer of all Antwerp. The arrival of Pilsner, then the rise of the numerous specialty beers has had no effect : it is this very characteristic amber that the inhabitants of the metropolis prefer. However, that doesn't mean one should think that it remains locked within the city gates. De Koninck is exported too : within memory it has even been encountered in certain remote corners of Hungary ...

Many times enlarged, renovated and modernised over the years, the brewery continues to be the pride of the master-brewers, who ply their trade with the same passion as on the first day. Today, it is the fifth generation of the Van den Boogaert family that holds the reins of the business.

De Koninck "Bolleke"

Top fermentation – Ale

🐝 golden amber

🏭 Brouwerij De Koninck, Antwerpen (Anvers)

% 5

Tasting notes

"De Koninck" is an amber beer with a short-lived head. It releases no gasses. It offers a fresh and malty nose, accompanied by a slight marine odour. Its flavour, also malty, presents very little bitterness. It is accompanied by notes of cinnamon as well as a light flavour of roasting that quickly disappears.

De Koninck (Cuvée)

Top fermentation – Ale

🐝 amber

🏭 Brouwerij De Koninck, Antwerpen (Anvers)

% 8

Tasting notes

The "Cuvée" presents a nice amber colour but its head is hardly abundant and doesn't hold well. Its fruity and acidic nose has Port accents. A little piquant in the mouth, it develops a nice, prolonged bitterness, notes of caramel, barley, a winy flavour and a light flavour of roasting.

Pub secret

Born in 1993, to celebrate the year dedicated to culture in the city of Antwerp, the Cuvée was an immediate hit, and took advantage of that to install itself as the number two beer from the De Koninck brewery. Take note that in 1999 a third beer, blond this time, named Antoon, has appeared to celebrate the 400th anniversary of the birth of the painter A. Van Dyck. It has a good chance of becoming an enviable success as well.

Delirium *(s. brewery p.130)*

Delirium tremens: n.m. *state of fevered agitation, trembling of the appendages, hallucination and troubled consciousness, attributable to alcoholic intoxication.* It is often in this state that we begin to see pink elephants, like those found on the labels of *Delirium* bottles. Somewhat surprising, isn't it, from a brewery, in this time where there is a strong insistence on the dangers of over consumption of alcoholic beverages ? Not really, since it is meant to be very tongue-in-cheek and is well said, at that : a little joking never hurt anyone. And though the managers at Huyghe, where *Delirium* is brewed, have done all they can to get us talking about their product as a fetish, it isn't warranted since we are faced with a beer of very fine manufacture. Take care though, the jovial character of the packaging (the bottle itself is fairly unique) shouldn't make you forget that you are sitting in front of a beer weighing in at 9%.

We can also pin on the Huyghe brewery, which has existed since 1654 – rarely bested – that they offer an impressive series of beers with regional characters, but with an unfortunately limited distribution. But that doesn't mean they can't be found since 65% of the total production is destined for export, leaving just a third of the *Delirium* at home.

At the end of 1999, *Delirium Tremens*, which was celebrating

Brasserie Huyghe - Van Melle
Brusselsesteenweg, 282 – 9090 Melle
Tel. : (32) 9 252 15 01 – Fax : (32) 9 252 29 31

its ten years of good and loyal service, welcomed the arrival of the intoxicating *Delirium Nocturnum*. Substantially identical in fabrication and philosophy, it differs in its dark colour. To be reserved for pleasant evenings... Finally, over those ten years the quantity produced by the Huyghe brewery tripled. Mostly thanks to its wandering brews, available in 36 different countries throughout the world, including Japan, Australia and Chile.

Delirium Nocturnum

Top fermentation – Other

🍺 mahogany brown

🏭 Brouwerij Huyghe, Melle (East Flanders)

% 9

Tasting notes

A beer with a dark brown colour, topped with a light brown head, both firm and persistent. It develops aromas of caramel, mocha and chocolate as well as liquorice. In the mouth, it delivers a certain softness but also power. Its bitterness becomes more and more pronounced throughout, and in proportion to, its drinking.

🍴 wild mushrooms, pheasant à la brabançonne.

Pub secret

In 1997, Delirium Tremens was proclaimed "Best Beer in the World" by specialists. Something worthy of note!

Delirium Tremens

Top fermentation – Other

🍺 coppery blond

🍺 Brouwerij Huyghe, Melle (East Flanders)

% 9

Tasting notes

Conceived with three different yeasts, it presents a beautiful colour, blond and coppery, as well as a compact and abundant head. The release of gasses is weak. It has a nose of wheat and barley with traces of coriander and orange. Delirium approaches the palate well and is slightly piquant. Full and round in the mouth, it is also spicy and has a pleasant bitterness.

🍽 hare's saddle, venison in pepper sauce, Vieux-Bruges cheese.

Double Enghien *(s. brewery p.133)*

In 1975, the Silly's small family business bought an old brewery in the neighbouring village, Enghien, held since 1858 by the Tennstedt-Decroes family. That was the point of departure for a renewal of the Hainaut brewing concern because it also took up the production of its neighbour, the Double Brown, to which was added, with the help of its popularity, a blond sister in 1992.

Today, these two twins are the heart of the production from the Silly Brewery (once Meynsbrughen Brewery) founded in 1850 and today directed by representatives of the fifth generation. As for the origin of the original Double's success, it dates, in part, from the period when the workers in Enghien took the tram to work in the coalfields in the area of Centre. The brewery was just a few feet from the terminus...

Also of interest, in 1947 the brewing activities far outstripped the agriculture, and since 1950 the Van Der Haegen family has settled into the task of producing a Pilsner, that they still brew today, even though the tide has definitely turned towards special beers. Since 1990, outside of the production of a white beer, Titje, the brewery has made a point of pride out of their opening up to external markets : it has been gratified by some international rewards as well.

The directors of this brewery, one of the last to produce a Pilsner outside of the star market performers, also intend to market another *Double Enghien.* It will be a beer re-fermented in the bottle and a little stronger than the classic *Double.*

Double Enghien Blonde *(s. brewery p.133)*

Top fermentation – Other

🍺 blond

🍺 Brasserie de Silly, Silly (Hainaut)

% 7,5

Tasting notes

Presenting a nice copper-blond body, the Double Enghien Blond develops an abundant head that holds well, and a substantial release of gasses. In the nose there is malt and hops, in the mouth as well, where these flavours are joined by a pleasant, prolonged but balanced, bitterness. Sweet, it offers a hint of caramel and notes of pear.

🍽 grilled mullet

Double Enghien Brune

Top fermentation – Other

🎨 auburn

🏭 Brasserie de Silly, Silly (Hainaut)

% 8

Tasting notes

This amber brown offers an abundant foam that doesn't hold long and an average release of gasses. The nose presents some fruity touches, sweet-sour, with red fruit accents and a hint of malt and yeast. In the mouth, it is a little piquant, sweet, and shows a light roasting, touches of mocha, liquorice and a late bitterness that is slightly dry.

Pub secret

We know that during World War One, the German army was constantly in need of copper to make munitions, most breweries and distilleries were "requested" to deliver their vats. The Silly brewery escaped being dismantled by a somewhat funny subterfuge. The owners had the idea to paint the vats black, to hide the metal that made them. This trick allowed them to continue to produce beer, but not to escape yet another type of requisitioning, since the brewery was charged with brewing for its fellow colleagues, themselves having been destroyed.

Duvel *(s. brewery p.128)*

For centuries, the brewing families have had a "habit", as is done among the nobility, of marrying among themselves. The Moortgat family, rather than choosing marriage, preferred "expatriation" since they were from the same village in the Brabant as the founders of Palm. All that to describe the passion that fermented in Jan-Leonard Moortgat in 1871. In 1923 his sons, who had taken up the family cause, delivered a beer that provoked as a first reaction from a baker in Breendonck "Duvel!". In the local vernacular, this means simply "The Devil". Though the beginning was difficult, Duvel is today one of the special Belgian beers the most popular abroad and the top fermented blond with the highest consumption in our kingdom. The brewery, that also produces Maredsous and other more private beers, pumps out 2.400.000 containers of Duvel each year.

More a phenomenon of society than a fashion phenomenon, Duvel has recently allowed the brewery to enter the stock market (where it is often high priced) and, at the same time, to change its name : the Moortgat Brewery has therefore become Duvel-Moortgat.

As for its characteristic flavour, an artistic success, it is principally due to a fermentation of several weeks at low temperature, preceded by a stay in a warm room, without which Duvel would not be a top fermented beer. Next, the brewer adds a small amount of fresh yeast to ensure re-fermentation in the bottle.

Duvel

Top fermentation – Other

🎨 blond

🏭 Brouwerij Duvel-Moortgat, Breendonck (Anvers)

% 8,5

Duvel

Tasting notes

A blond beer with a beautiful gold light, Duvel is re-fermented in the bottle. It is characterised by a white head, compact and tenacious, and aromas of barley and hops. In the mouth, it is round and dry, a little piquant with a prolonged and balanced bitterness. There is a hint of orange zest, pear and green apple.

Pub secret

Amateurs know well the story of the origin of the name "Duvel". What they might not know is that at the bottom of their glass sleeps a little bit of English Ale. Albert Moortgat, who wanted above all to produce a high quality beer, travelled to Scotland in the hopes of finding yeast. It was hard work, that's the least we can write, but our man succeeded in procuring a small jug-full of yeast.

That same yeast is what is still used today because this type of fermentation never completely ceases.

A new beer (which we didn't have time to taste before wrapping up) has just been created by Duvel-Moortgat in association with the Passendale creamery. According to a survey, the majority of people associate the cheese with the Passendale beer, although the beer never had been released. So, the dream had to be made into reality ... a feat finally accomplished today.

Ename *(s. brewery p.133)*

The region called the "Flemish Ardennes" enjoys a long and rich brewing history. One can still find a series of undiluted, family owned breweries. Many documents attest to the existence of the Roman Brewery from 1545, and Louis Roman is today, the twelfth generation of an imposing lineage, rarely bested! How then, under such conditions, do they weather the modern demand for all special beers ? Some old ruins nearby and an excellent iron-rich spring water in the basement give the impulse necessary to produce these beers of character, with lots of head.

Ename Tripel

Top fermentation – Abbey

🍺 golden blond

📷 Brouwerij Roman, Mater (East Flanders)

% 9

Tasting notes

Limpid, this coppery blond develops a head that is abundant and compact, that holds well. It has a considerable release of gasses. It presents a fruity and complex nose, lingering equally over malt and hops. A fine acidity, notes of caramel, malt, a nice roasted flavour, accents of liquorice, anis, mocha and pear all define its impression in the mouth. It finishes with a prolonged and balanced bitterness.

Pub secret

The history of the abbey of Ename, in the area of Oudenaarde (Audenarde), is somewhat shocking. The Benedictine monastery St Salvator (Saint-Sauver) was founded in 1063. Erected on the banks of the Escaut river, it disappeared, swallowed up by the river after a sudden natural shift in its course. For once, the revolutionaries had nothing to do with it ...

Fruit Défendu (s. brewery p.131)

"Fruit Défendu" (Forbidden Fruit) is the top of the line product from the Hoegaarden brewery. It is also the highest in alcohol and the least known. It does everything to get people talking about it. Its name, of course, which makes an obvious reference to the heaven on Earth wasted by Adam and Eve; its label, inspired by a work of Rubens ; its glass, with a foot that resembles a serpent, which enabled Eve's blunder. Its colour, would rather call to mind a fine wine that had aged for some time.

Fruit Défendu

Top fermentation – Other

🍺 red brown, very dark

📷 Brouwerij De Kluis, Hoegaarden (Flemish Brabant)

% 9

MTasting notes

Forbidden Fruit spreads its dark red colour under a fine head that is white and compact. In the nose, one senses principally aromas of spiced hops. Its flavour, perfectly balanced between sweet and dry, leads to a roundness due to coriander and a grand aromatic complexity (coffee, apricot, almond, apple, ...). It ends with a bitter, dry finish.

Pub secret

What could the beers brewed at Hoegaarden have in common ? First of all, nothing seems similar among a white beer, a "Grand Cru", or a "Fruit Defendu" : neither their colour, alcohol content, brewing process or much less their origins. Yet still, isn't there some little familiar after-taste ? If fact, you've found it – coriander and curacao (a bitter orange) figure in the make up of each product of the "De Kluis" brewery ... a sort of trademark !

Gauloise (La) *(s. brewery p.123)*

Gauloise is the beer that made the du Bocq brewery's reputation, located at Purnode (Yvoir) in the Dinant region. In other pursuits, it also produces several other beers of a regional or craft character, and is the appointed broker for a small number of other breweries. But the Gauloise distinguishes itself from the other members of the family by the fact that it has been around since the origin of the brewery, of which it is a veritable product. Once again, it was agricultural pursuits that gave this brewery a start, under the direction of the Belot family. At the head of this brewery since 1858, it is already under the fifth generation. The Gauloise was born one fine morning, in the peace re-discovered after World War One and benefited from pristine water. For years it was made only in a dark version, but 1994 saw two other versions appear : a blond and an amber. The three varieties are drunk from a beautiful glass, a sort of designer "*chope*" (mug).

A member of that rarefied group of large Belgian breweries that remain independent, it produces around 100.000 hectolitres per year and exports to most of the neighbouring countries.

Gauloise Ambrée (La)

Top fermentation – Other

🍺 amber

🏠 Brasserie du Bocq, Purnode (Namur)

% 6,5

Tasting notes

This limpid amber develops an abundant, long-lasting head, as well as a significant release of gasses. It offers a nose of malt and hops underlined by smoky notes. In the mouth, it reveals a light roasting, flavours of malt and notes of orange blossom. One senses a pleasant bitterness, slightly dry, and a taste of coriander and anis. Known as a "vicious beer" it is important to be cautious when opening the bottle.

🍴 grilled chops

Pub secret

An author and amateur beer taster wrote of the first-born from the du Bocq brewery that it had aromas marked by ... tobacco. So then, does it follow logically that it is called Gauloise Blonde... ?

Gauloise Blonde (La)

Top fermentation – Other

🍺 bright yellow blond

🏠 Brasserie du Bocq, Purnode (Namur)

% 7

Tasting notes

A golden blond beer, that develops an abundant head, holding well and also producing a significant release of gasses. Gauloise Blonde has a nose of malt and hops, characteristics that are also found, though more gentle, in the flavour, accompanied by notes of bay laurel. In the mouth, it is equally round and develops a prolonged bitterness.

(ɪɪɪ) mixed kebab

Gauloise Brune (La)
Top fermentation – Other
🍺 dark fawn
🛕 Brasserie du Bocq, Purnode (Namur)
% 8,5

Tasting notes
A light brown, top fermented, created between the Wars, it is sweeter but more "unique" than its blond sister brew, notably thanks to the aromas of liquorice and caramel. It delivers an abundant head that holds well, as well as a significant release of gasses. Malty to the nose, it is slightly piquant in the mouth, with light roasting, liquorice and pear flavours backing it up. There is also a noticeable, prolonged and well-balanced bitterness.

(ɪɪɪ) grilled chops

Grimbergen (s. brewery p.122)
Like all the abbeys of Belgium and elsewhere founded in the Middle Ages, Grimbergen has not escaped numerous invasions and reconstructions. Founded in 1128 by Saint Norbert, who also presided over the destinies of Leffe, it was favoured by the Berthouts, lords of the region, against the will of the Dukes of Brabant. Unfortunately, because of a lack of monks, its construction was never completed ; there remains only the abbey church, dating from the XVIIth century. *Burned but not destroyed*, as stipulated in its Latin motto written on its bottles, a motto befitting a Phœnix, guarantees continuity and revolution. Unable to be brewed at its abbey,

Grimbergen was raised again to honour by Alken-Maes and remains (a well earned title) one of the most highly valued "specials" in Belgium.

Grimbergen Blonde
Top fermentation – Other
🍺 blond
🛕 Brasserie de l'Union, Jumet (Hainaut)
% 6,5

Tasting notes
Presenting a beautiful "old gold" colour and developing a light head, white and short lived, Grimbergen Blonde has a fruity and balanced nose. Its approach is a little piquant.

Pub secret
The history of Grimbergen is decidedly lively because after the invasions, with their well known effects, it was the beer that had to face up to a move in 1978. Brewed at Waarloos (in the province of Anvers), it was transferred to Jumet (Charleroi) with the purchase of the L'Union brewery by Alken-Maes.

Grimbergen Dubbel
Top fermentation – Abbey
🍺 red brown
🛕 Brasserie de l'Union, Jumet (Hainaut)
% 6,5

Tasting notes
The deep brown body has highlights of red. It is topped by a compact head, that is short lived and releases an average effervescence. To the nose, it carries mainly mocha and barley, while in the mouth it is full, a little dry and soft. It also offers flavours of roasting, anis

and liquorice. It leaves a nice bitterness, balanced and fairly short.

🍴 escalope cordon bleu, tagliatelle with mushroom-cream sauce

Grimbergen Optimo Bruno

Top fermentation – Abbey

🍺 amber

🏭 Brasserie de l'Union, Jumet (Hainaut)

% 10

Tasting notes

Originally, this was an Easter beer, but it is now brewed year round. Under a creamy head, abundant and long-lived, it presents a clear brown colour with red highlights. Lacking some power in the nose, it is distinguished by a balance in the mouth, with lingering anis, liquorice and pear flavours and finishing with a light bitterness.

🍴 filet American

Grimbergen Tripel

Top fermentation – Abbey

🍺 amber blond

🏭 Brasserie de l'Union, Jumet (Hainaut)

% 9

Tasting notes

Grimbergen Triple is a golden blond with a significant release of gasses. It develops a beautiful strong head. It is a soft beer with background notes of orange and caramel. In the mouth, it is characterised by a flavour of malt and complex spices, accompanied by fresh hops. Round, it pours forth a fresh bitterness, underlined by notes of honey and vanilla. Slightly dry in the final stage.

Grisette *(s. brewery p.129)*

Grisette was, in the beginning, a beer to be drunk early, mostly at everyday meals in the region of the Centre. Racked into wooden barrels, its vocation was to quench the thirst of its drinkers. Production waned little by little with the introduction of the Pilsners and other table beers. Despite an incredible capacity to chase thirst, especially in the summer, it fell into complete abandon, before being "re-brewed", in a confidential process, by the De Smedt brewery in Opwijk (Brabant Flamand). But, a beer that originated in the Centre should be brewed in the Centre. This was undoubtedly what the Friart family was thinking when they took up the production of Grisette two or three years ago.

At the same time, this amber with an abundant head celebrated the birth of two little sisters, the pretty Blonde and the refreshing Blanche (White). And, after having known the joys of the table, then darker times, Grisette has become a beer of celebrations, notably in accompaniment to the rhythmic hammering of the sabots in Gilles. Agreeably unique, it is unfiltered, re-fermented in the bottle and is drunk cold. It is also distinguished by being lower in alcohol than the majority of top fermented beers.

Grisette Ambrée

Top fermentation – Other

🍺 amber

🏭 Brasserie Friart, Le Roeulx (Hainaut)

% 5

Tasting notes

Grisette "classique" – the strongest and more unique of the trilogy – presents an amber body, limpid, with an average release of gasses. It is topped by a compact and long lasting head. In the nose, one senses above all barley and hops, as well as an herby note. Round in the mouth, it reveals flavours of yeast and hops.

🍽 breaded veal, pasta

Gulden Draak *(s. brewery p.137)*

Top fermentation - Special
🍺 brown red
🏭 Brouwerij Van Steenberge, Gent (East Flanders)
% 10,5

Tasting notes

Treasures are protected by a dragon in every fairy tale. This treasure of a beer is an adventure, and needs experienced beer drinkers to slay the dragon. The dark color of that barley wine is an exception among the Belgian triples. This beer is refermented in the bottle and in the keg. Gulden Draak balances a natural malt, toffee-like sweetness, with a mellow happiness and some "hoppy" accents. The aroma is round, very complex, sweet, and hides the high alcohol content. It is a dessert on its own, or an ideal companion for a chocolate cake. Share this beer with your significant other, and all you'll need is each other.

The statue of the Gulden Draak was donated by a Norwegian king, during one of the first crusades in the 11th century, to the city of Constantinople (Istanbul). About 100 years later, a Fleming became Emperor of Constantinople, liked the statue and brought it home. Today it sits on top of the Belfry of Ghent, where it protects the treasures of the city.

Hapkin *(s. brewery p.132)*

Brewed since 1982, Hapkin is a beer with a firm character. Its name comes from the local argot and means *"cut"* or *"chopped"*, a nickname attributed to Baudouin de Flandre in the XIIth century who always carried a small hatchet attached to his belt. But we also find, to our amusement, that "Hopkin" is one of the derivative names from the Dutch *hop*, which means ... hops! And the native region of this pulpy blond abounds with hops to such a degree that it seems to breathe and taste like its lupuline extract, to no end. This is, of course, the spice that gives this beer its refined perfume. From there you can imagine the small step to the word games that follow. But, return for a moment to 900 or so years in the past. At that time, the famous and renowned Baudouin insisted that the brothers of the Ter Duinen abbey produce a blond beer with a character that would encourage his troops to feel like they were invincible... so, they brewed the ancestor of today's Hapkin.

For the past few years, this beer has been the mascot product of Jan-Baptist Louwaege, fifth generation in this family of father-to-son brewers. His grandfather, Placide Louwaege, abandoned agriculture in 1877 to develop his other interests in brewing. The vocation of working the earth is still present on the label of the Flandrian, the other tap product of the Louwaeges. But since the arrival of Jan-Baptiste and Frédéric Louwaege, the brewing has focused on the Hapkin, which has grown by 20% per year since 1993. It is destined primarily for the market in Flanders, but is equally present in the Netherlands and in France. And a few years from now, we will see it on the market in England and Germany as well.

Hapkin

Top fermentation – Other

🍺 golden blond

🏭 Brouwerij Louwaege, Kortemarkt (West Flanders)

% 8,5

Tasting notes

Lightly malted, the golden blond from the Louwaege brewery offers a compact, tenacious and abundant head. It is a highly perfumed beer, boldly fruity and supple. It is slightly piquant and distinguishes itself with well-presented flavours of hops. It has a marked, balanced acidity, and a somewhat dry finish.

🍽 mussels, eel "au vert"

Pub secret

Among the beers with more limited diffusion from the Louwaege brewery, there is one called Akila. It is simply the Flemish transposition of the Latin term "aquila" meaning eagle. Befitting, considering the name of the brewery before it was purchased by Placide Louwaege was ... "Den Arend", meaning "the eagle".

Hoegaarden Grand Cru *(s. brewery p.131)*

It's true, it has all the points of a grand beer. And although it may profit by having the same name as its neighbour in the brewing vat, it has neither the same properties nor the same colour. It is in effect, a blond, top fermented, with individual characteristics, and with more than just quenching thirst as its goal. It is equally appropriate to celebratory occasions, but performs in a less peremptory way than the Blanche. A Grand Cru is drunk calmly, as its tailored glass suggests. Its relatively high level of alcohol and its very complex flavour, a flavour truly evolving only with time, don't allow a large

amount to be drunk in one sitting, that not being its purpose.

Hoegaarden Grand Cru

Top fermentation – Other

🍺 golden blond with lees

📛 Brouwerij De Kluis, Hoegaarden (Flemish Brabant)

% 8,7

Tasting notes

A cloudy beer brewed without wheat, Hoegaarden Grand Cru offers its nose of barley and yeast through a white, short-lived head. The release of gasses is weak. Full in the mouth, it delivers a pleasant taste of hops, presupposing a long bitterness a lightly sweet fruitiness and a powerful aroma that recalls peaches.

Pub secret

If you want to understand the breadth and depth of the history of Hoegaarden (the brewery and also its town and surroundings), take note that there is now a work entirely devoted to this. "Het Land van Hoegaarden", that's its name, explores the White Beer and what made it such a success, but also the other "outputs" of the family, from cooking recipes to an in-depth exploration of the region, via behind the scenes tours. The only "black mark" for the book is that it is currently only available in Dutch. Here's hoping that versions in French and English are forthcoming.

Hoegaarden Spéciale (s. brewery p.131)

No doubt because it felt lonely, the Blanche aided in the birth of a "little sister" who, according to its qualities, is more like the eldest in the family. Presented with much trumpeting in the media, the "Speciale" is brewed from October to March but its presence in the beer aisle is quasi permanent. Its main characteristic is to be a White Beer... despite its golden blond colour. In that, it approaches the White Beers of yore, in which there was often as much to eat as to drink and which had an aroma and flavour clearly more pronounced. Though it is inevitably a member and class of the Hoegaarden family, it relies more on its aptitudes as a beer to be enjoyed while "cozied up around the fire" rather than a classic White Beer, whose festive character and "fun" side are not as strongly demonstrated.

Hoegaarden Speciale

Top fermentation – White beer

🍺 golden, cloudy

📛 Brouwerij De Kluis, Hoegaarden (Flemish Brabant)

% 5,6

Tasting notes

Often served between 2 and 5°C, Hoegaarden Speciale is equally agreeable to drink at 9-10°C during the Winter season. It is a golden blond lightly spiced and releasing a pronounced odour of coriander and tobacco. Speciale also offers aromas of wheat, fresh spices, a touch of citrus and a light bitterness. Round in the mouth, it develops a taste of malt lightly roasted, lifted up by notes of honey and hazelnut.

Joseph Spelt Ale (s. brewery p.133)

Top fermentation – White

🍺 pale
🏭 Brasserie de Silenrieux (Province of Namur)
% 5

Tasting notes

There is no question that Joseph is a Belgian wheat beer. This is obvious by its cloudy look, the way it feels in the mouth, and aroma. However, the taste of that organic beer sets it apart from the commercially known Belgian wheat beers. Spelt is the ancestor of the wheat family (wheat is 'spelta' in Latin). It's getting new attention nowadays, especially by people who like health food—non processed, organic food. Contrary to regular wheat, spelt is pretty much still the same as it was many centuries ago. It's also called 'poor man's wheat', and it can grow on poorer grounds, such as the grounds that are patched in between the woods around Silenrieux. The Joseph is slightly fruity, and has a very pale color with a beautiful bright white head. Although you can pour a nice, clear looking glass of Joseph, it is recommended to roll or slightly shake the bottle before opening, to serve a more cloudy glass of this refreshing and unfiltered beer. Joseph goes very well with salads, and with seafood.

Judas *(s. brewery p.122)*

Contrary to what its name might lead you to think, this blond is completely frank and doesn't hide its true intentions. Instead, it leaves a very positive impression and a souvenir of agreeable moments spent in its company. Born in 1986 in the area of Waregem (West Flanders) in the care of the Zulte brewery, since then coming under the direction of the Alken-Maes group, it is today produced at Pays Noir, in the greater Charleroi area. With a relatively discrete diffusion, Judas merits the effort to find it, even if only to appreciate its beautiful bottle and head of inimitable thickness.

Judas

Top fermentation – Other
🍺 golden blond
🏭 Brasserie de l'Union, Jumet (Hainaut)
% 8,5

Tasting notes

The "Judas" reveals a beautiful blond-gold colour and an abundant head that holds well. There is a significant release of gasses. In the nose, it delivers aromas of barley and hops, accompanied by a note of fruit. Piquant and very round in the mouth, the barley and hops are present again. A few herby accents don't hurt this fresh and well balanced beer, slightly citrus in its finish trimmed with dried orange.

Julius *(s. brewery p.130)*

Julius Cesar, though we don't know what he said of the Belgian people, preferred beer to wine. That's how the story goes today, anyway. It is for that reason, undoubtedly, that a beer pays him homage, more than two thousand years later. A top fermented blond among many others, it is a pure product from ... the Interbrew brewing empire. Coincidence? Still today the brewing landscape of Belgium is littered with "great names of history": Julius, Napoleon, Carolus, Godefroy, ...

Julius
Top fermentation – Other

🍺 golden blond

📷 Brouwerij De Kluis, Hoegaarden (Flemish Brabant)

% 8,8

Tasting notes

Made using three types of hops, this "old gold" blond beer, with the veiled body, has a soft approach, a fruity bouquet and a dry after-taste. When ideally served (between 5 and 6°C), it develops a beautiful compact head that holds well. There is an average release of gasses, a fruity nose, with wafts of barley and wheat. In the mouth, there is a taste of caramel, roasted malt and a nice persistent bitterness, completed by a touch of spice and a complex aroma.

Jupiler *(s. brewery p.130)*

Jupiler, it needs no further introduction ! Is it really necessary to linger over the most consumed "man's" beer in Belgium ? A beer for everyday and for grand occasions as well (sporting events, student parties, ...), "Jupe" is more than a beer, its an institution. It was born one fine day in September 1966 under the appellation Jupiler 5, at the Piedboeuf brewery in Jupille (Liège), well known at that time for its light table beers. Its success was so lightening quick that in 1968 it had already taken the number two position on the Belgian sales charts. Its entry under the Interbrew group only accelerated its rise and assured its notoriety. Long live Jupiler !

Jupiler
Bottom fermentation – Pilsner

🍺 blond

📷 Brasserie Interbrew, Jupille (Liège)

% 5,2

Tasting notes

Blond Pilsner, "Jupe" shines its golden rays out from under a light head of foam. The release of gasses is significant and the bubbles are abundant. Barley has a strong presence in the nose. It is a slightly piquant beer, thirst quenching, with a final, short bitterness and notes of fine hops.

Pub secret

There is an amusing Flemish expression used to characterise a strong beer. They say a beer has *a bull's hoof*. Bizarre, since the Piedboeuf (literally – *bull's-foot*) brewery (the family name of its founders) makes, in addition to Jupiler, beers with some of the lowest volumes of alcohol !

Jupiler N.A.
Bottom fermentation – N.A.

🍺 blond

📷 Brouwerij Interbrew, Leuven (Flemish Brabant)

% 0,1

Tasting notes

Golden blond beer, with the same title as its famous sister, its head is short lived even though there is a significant release of gasses. Nose : aromas of malt, in the mouth : again, malt, a light bitterness and notes of ... honey.

🍴 light cheese

Kasteel Bier *(s. brewery p.137)*

Those who know and appreciate "Bière du Château" rest assured, they can still find their favourite under the unique appellation Kasteel Bier". The term "Bière du Château" is a relic from the time when the father of today's chief thought it would be easier to penetrate the Walloon market by addressing the potential customers in French. But today the marketing strategies have taken another turn. The Van Honsebrouk brewery is today turning towards Europe and producing their publicity materials (labels, coasters, signage, ...) in the two languages became difficult, even more so since Kasteel is very attached to its territory and origins. So much for the short history. As for the publicity itself, it has been proclaiming loud and strong for some time : "The richest beer in Belgium...". And, you can't deny that these two beers have aristocratic roots. Not everyone has the chance to claim lordly parentage.

Since 1989, these brews steeped in nobility, have ripened slowly in the caves of the Ingelmunster chateau, not far from the Lys, 6 to 12 weeks for the brown. It has the more model characteristics of the two, and is often compared, as much for its flavour as for its "philosophy", to a fine Port. It should be tasted calmly, far from all agitation. Collectors of coasters will take delight, too, in adding the giant *Kasteel* to their collection.

Kasteel Bier Gouden Tripel

Top fermentation – Other

🍺 golden yellow
🏭 Brouwerij Van Honsebrouck, Ingelmunster (West Flanders)
% 11

Tasting notes

The golden blond of Ingelmunster develops a thin head that doesn't hold well, along with a weak release of gasses. The nose blends herby notes with those of fresh hops. There is also an aroma of roasting. Soft and round in the mouth, it is piquant and delivers a prolonged bitterness that slightly interferes with some accents of dry fruit and port.

Pub secret

A beer that assuredly keeps well, Kasteel even supplies, on its label, an indication of the vintage of fabrication, as if to make it seem even more like a fine wine. Information to make its conservation in your cave a little easier ...

Kasteel Bier Ingelmunster

Top fermentation – Other

🍺 deep brown
🏭 Brouwerij Van Honsebrouck, Ingelmunster (West Flanders)
% 11

Tasting notes

A dark brown beer, it is topped with a cream coloured head, abundant and short lived. It has an average release of gasses. To the nose, it presents aromas of barley and a real sweetness. In the mouth, it is round and full, slightly piquant and developing notes of roasting, mocha, liquorice and banana, while revealing a pleasant, prolonged bitterness.

🍴 filet of wild boar, Passendale cheese

Kwak *(s. brewery p.123)*

Although Kwak is a very agreeable beer to drink, one must admit that its famous "coachman's glass" is the element that characterises it best. This glass, in the shape of a flared test tube, bulged out at the bottom and held in a wooden rack, is distinctive to say the least. It was used by postal coachmen, circulating around Malines and Gand, who stopped to quaff a pint at Pauwel Kwak's inn. Since a law from the Napoleonic code forbade coachmen and their passengers to descend from their carriage to consume beer, this ingenious system still permitted them to quench their thirst. And so, a small piece of wood attached to the coach at the height of a standing man, gave the innkeeper a chance to attach the glass to the harnessing... As for the shape of the glass, it permitted no spillage, even while the horse was travelling at a fast pace and over rough tracks. The Bosteels brewery restored this beautiful amber beer to honour, and kept its distinctive elements.

La Binchoise *(s. brewery p.131)*

The ramparts of Binche were recently restored. They have become the largest complex of Belgian fortifications that encircle a city and integrate into a vast tourism project centred on the city of Gilles. At the foot of these ramparts the "Binchoise" brewery perfectly reflects the reinvigoration of the city. It all started "for pleasure" : André Graux, in the early 80s, was making fruit wines in microscopic quantities for a small circle of friends. A few years later, in 1986, our man and his wife found themselves unemployed. So the idea came to them to brew some beer, more to use up their time than to realise any profit. The least you can say is that their plan took, and very shortly a move to a site that better fit their burgeoning pursuits appeared necessary.

The couple bought some used equipment and installed them-

Don't leave Binche without seeing its brewery.

BRASSERIE
LA BINCHOISE

FAUBOURG SAINT PAUL, 38
B-7130 BINCHE - BELGIUM
PHONE AND FAX:(32) 64 33 61 86

selves into an ancient malting house : the "Binchoise" brewery was born. Without any real previous experience, though the proprietor's father was a chemical engineer, the enterprise was immediately crowned with success. A Gold Medal at the annual international competition in Chicago in 1995 can be considered a veritable consecration ... and as recognition from their peers. In 1999, the Graux family, who employ several full time people, hired a brewing engineer. And, in this brewery where they promote a family, though not amateur, atmosphere, the directors are investing in renovation and expansion of their facilities in order to more easily and regularly welcome visitors. A beautiful tasting room was just created to that end.

One should also know that the Binchoise played the role of a precursor ; its "parents" were the first to dare mix honey into the Belgian's favourite beverage to create the aptly named "Bear's Beer". Add to that the classic blonds and browns, the Noël special, and the Springtime beer that we taste with so much pleasure. Binchoise is present, along with others, in all the city cafés and is inevitably associated with the Mardi Gras carnival : the Gille drawn on the label attests to this. But don't let that keep you from drinking it at other times of the year ...

La Binchoise Blonde
Top fermentation – Other
🍺 straw yellow, slightly cloudy
🏭 Brasserie La Binchoise, Binche (Hainaut)
% 6,5

Tasting notes
This golden blond develops an abundant head that holds well and a significant release of gasses. It offers an herby nose, stamped with malt and hops. In the mouth, it is acidic, bringing a flavour of malt and orange blossom and presents a nice, balanced and prolonged bitterness.

Lambic (Geuze)
Spontaneous fermentation – Gueuze
🍺 coppery gold
🏭 Brasserie Cantillon, Anderlecht (Bruxelles)
% 5

Tasting notes
The Cantillon Gueuze, preferably served at 12-15°C, presents a beautiful golden blond body. It develops an abundant head, but it doesn't hold well. To the nose, it releases characteristic, rustic aromas of Lambic and fruit. In the mouth, it is first acidic, then sour and finally bitter. Its acidity is relatively balanced.
🍴 cream cheese tartine, cheese tart

Lambic (Kriek)
Spontaneous fermentation – Kriek (Cherry)
🍺 deep red
🏭 Brasserie Cantillon, Anderlecht (Bruxelles)
% 5

Tasting notes
A red head, abundant and short-lived, tops a body coloured carmine red. To the nose, the odour is very characteristic : cherry and pip, wood and Lambic. The nose is slightly

winy. Very acidic in the mouth, it develops a pronounced flavour of cherry, not at all sugary and a nice sourness. There is also a fresh, bitter after-taste.

🍴 cherry duck, cherry tart.

Leffe (s. brewery p.130)

... *et la vie prend tout son goût*! A third place in the highly contested special beers market and fifth position in notoriety among all Belgian beers : the least we can write is that Leffe does well for itself. Perceived as the perfect companion for pleasant moments, or so the wave of publicity with its eloquent images would have us think, the beer's past, and even more so that of its abbey, is studded with periods of trouble.

Having arrived at the banks of the Meuse, near Dinant in 1152, the canons of the Prémontrés order settled there, despite diverse wars, up until... the Revolution. At this time, the community disappeared, and the buildings were put up for sale, then became a glass factory. The site was returned to its original use in 1903, when ecclesiastics from the province occupied the buildings for 20 or so years, before ceding the place to the canons of Tongerlo. A few years later (1931), the Leffe Abbey regained its independence. It survives today thanks to federal subsidies and profits from brewing, confided for some time already to the Interbrew group.

Leffe Blonde

Top fermentation – Abbey

🍺 golden, almost amber

🏭 Brouwerij Interbrew, Leuven (Flemish Brabant)

% 6,5

Tasting notes

Leffe Blonde develops a nice compact head that doesn't hold long, which tops a golden body, slightly amber. Its powerful nose caches perfumes of malted barley and wheat. Round in the mouth, it develops a prolonged bitterness and a weak release of gasses. Its flavour is fairly smoky with notes of tobacco, prune and spices. It seems more alcoholic in its finish and reveals then notes of cedar wood.

Leffe Brune

Top fermentation – Abbey

🍺 dark brown

🏭 Brouwerij Interbrew, Leuven (Flemish Brabant)

% 6,3

Tasting notes

A dark brown colour, it develops a light head that doesn't linger and a fruity nose. It is a beer that is simultaneously soft and round, with a good approach.

Leffe Radieuse

Top fermentation – Abbey

🍺 red brown

🏭 Brouwerij Interbrew, Leuven (Flemish Brabant)

% 8,2

Tasting notes

Leffe Radieuse presents a compact and abundant head, that holds well. After its nose of herbs and barley, this soft beer, pleasant in the mouth, offers a flavour of roasted coffee, a balanced yet short bitterness and traces of toasted bread.

🍴 Herve cheese (not blue)

Pub secret

Leffe Radieuse takes its name, according to its creators, from the resplendent aureole of a saint. It is also true that this beautiful brown has lit up more than one amateur in our pubs ! Like the others, it may be tasted in peace in a *Café Leffe*, the latest idea from the genial Interbrew group to raise its brew onto a pedestal. In fact, do you know what village was chosen as the site for the very first *Café Leffe* in the Walloon region? Dinant,... of course !

Leffe Triple

Top fermentation – Abbey
🍺 golden, clear brown
🏭 Brouwerij Interbrew, Leuven (Flemish Brabant)
% 8,4

Tasting notes

A top fermented beer, of a golden blond colour, its nose is fruity and complex, heightened by notes of wheat, barley, chickaree and coriander. It offers a nice compact head that holds well. Soft of flavour and piquant in the mouth, it develops a balanced bitterness, prolonged by herby aromas.

Liefmans *(s. brewery p.133)*

The Liefmans brewery has been in the most undulating region of Flanders (Oudenaarde) since 1679 and produces mostly the "brown" beers typical of that region. Aside from these classics, Liefmans, which has been an integral part of the Riva group since the beginning of the 90s, also brews a "Kriek" – that is, a top fermented brew infused with

cherries – which has the peculiarity of only being brewed for a short period in the winter, and which is consumed ... hot ! To draw a parallel with mulled wine, also heavy in tannins, is only a short hop, even though the level of alcohol is much lower and the spices used are different.

Liefmans Glühkriek

Top fermentation – Flemish Brown
🍺 dark brown/red
🏭 Brouwerij Liefmans, Oudenaarde (East Flanders)
% 6,5

Tasting notes

This beer presents a deep red body, a pronounced aroma of cherries, cloves, penetrating and intriguing anis, cinnamon and almond. Slightly sweet to the taste, it delivers a good amount of cherry flavour, added to that spices and aromatic herbs. In the finish, one notices a bitter touch. It is tasted when served at 70°C.

Lindemans *(s. brewery p.132)*

In 1809, the Lindemans family worked a farm in Vlezenbeek, a suburb of Brussels. In winter, to maintain a lucrative pursuit, the proprietors installed a small Lambic brewery. With the help of their success, the brewing activities became more and more important until, in 1930, the farming work was definitively abandoned.
The Gueuze and the Kriek were the first beers to see the light of day and, over the years, they helped to deliver other varieties on the same theme : Faro

(1978), Framboise *Raspberry* (1980), Cassis *Blackcurrant* (1986) and Pécheresse *Peach* (1987).

Holders of several honourable titles gleaned from various international concourses, the Lindemans family – today in the fourth generation – has quintupled its annual production in the space of 20 years (from 5000 to 25000 hectolitres). Outside of Belgium (45%), its principle markets are, notably, France, the United States, the Netherlands, Japan and Argentina.

Lindemans (Framboise)

Spontaneous fermentation – Raspberry

🍷 red - amber

📷 Brouwerij Lindemans, Vlezenbeek (Flemish Brabant)

% 3,5

Tasting notes

Lindemans' Framboise presents a beautiful red brown body and develops a weak head that is short lived. There is almost no release of gasses. In the nose, one discovers fruit (raspberry) and sweetness (syrup). To the taste, it is very sweet and acidic. There is an artificial raspberry flavour, notes of candy, wood and tobacco. There is almost no flavour of Lambic and it develops no bitterness.

Pub secret

In a moment of creativity and experimentation, the Lindemans brewery launched, in 1995, a Lambic infused with tea. It was a particularly acidic beer, but sweet at the same time. Unfortunately, we don't know if this new product made inroads in the marketplace in England... But if it did, there's little chance that the internet site, hopelessly unavailable (blank!) in its English version, had anything to do with it... !

Lindemans (Geuze)

Spontaneous fermentation – Gueuze

🍷 coppery

📷 Brouwerij Lindemans, Vlezenbeek (Flemish Brabant)

% 5

Tasting notes

Lindemans' Gueuze offers a weak head that doesn't hold long, its release of gasses is weak while its nose is fruity and sweet. Otherwise, its taste evokes little of a Lambic, and is closer to a Faro with its level of sugars and its absence of bitterness.

Lindemans (Kriek)

Spontaneous fermentation – Kriek (Cherry)

🍷 deep red

📷 Brouwerij Lindemans, Vlezenbeek (Flemish Brabant)

% 4

Tasting notes

A beautiful deep red body, a head compact but weak, rosy and short-lived, as well as a weak release of gasses sums up the visual qualities. In the nose, one finds fruity (cherry) and sugary (syrup) accents. Very sweet in flavour, it is also acidic and brings up cherry (artificial ?) and fruit stone elements. It has very little flavour of Lambic, is very sugary and offers no bitterness.

🍴 cherry tart

Maes *(s. brewery p.121)*

Spearhead of the Alken-Maes brewery (ex Danone Group, whose parts - 100% - were purchased by an English brewery), Maes completes the assembly of Belgium's most consumed beers, the first two market positions being held by the unassailable twin sisters of the Interbrew group. Born twenty years earlier than its Liège based competitor, we also find it at public events, and for the same reasons : wide production, thirst quenching character, conviviality,... Its essential peculiarity is that it is non-pasteurised. Aside from its classic products like Maes, the Alken group has permitted a whole series of smaller productions to appear, with more thrust than if they had evolved on their own.

It seems that the leaders of the brewery want to continue in this vein, aiming to capture as many of the market "niches" as possible (to wit, for example, Maes Cool and the other Maes Naturals). In the coming months, Alken-Maes will launch two new beers aimed primarily at pleasing the young, whose tastes pivot more around lemonades, colas, and energy drinks with their bizarre effects. We've been told that the rhythm may be two new products per year in this market sector.

On the distribution front, besides the presence of Maes in many football stadiums around the country, we've learned that an agreement has been undertaken with the American group Premium Parks. They, the proprietors of 35 amusement parks worldwide, have signed an exclusive contract with the number two Belgian brewer. This concerns the provision of beer to six parks, including Walibi and Bellewaerd in Belgium, but also the three French Walibis and Six-Flags in the Netherlands.

> The Alken-Maes group has a presence in the United Kingdom, where it opened cafés under the name The Belgian Monk.

Maes Pils

Bottom fermentation – Pilsner

🍺 clear blond

🏭 Brouwerij Alken-Maes, Waarloos (Anvers)

% 5,1

Tasting notes

The golden blond from the Alken-Maes brewery develops an abundant head that holds well and a significant release of gasses. Fairly neutral in the nose, one nonetheless senses the presence of malt. A sensation that is found also in the mouth, accompanied by a light bitterness. The finish is fairly neutral, despite a few notes of honey.

🍽 mussel casserole, plaice meunière

Pub secret

Théo Maes, president of the group until 1993, was one of very few Belgian brewers, or even Europeans, that could taste a beer that carried his name. If he had left his post a few years later, he would have gained, with pleasure no doubt, the title of "Fournisseur Breveté de la Cour" (Purveyor to the Royal Court), bestowed on the brewery in 1998.

Maredsous (s. brewery p.128)

Many people who grew up in the region of Namur or Charleroi will doubtless have fond memories of Sunday drives to Maredsous, bread, cheese, souvenir boutiques and ... a great beer for the grown-ups ! No doubt this is why, now that they have reached adulthood themselves, they repeat the cycle, this time with kids of their own. And, judging by the crowd witnessed there on a recent visit, the cycle isn't about to stop ! This Sunday pilgrimage *en masse* is actually relatively recent for, though the neo-gothic abbey itself was finished in 1881, the visitor's centre, which permits the monastic community to better participate in modern life, wasn't completed until 1948. The centre was also recently transferred to an area of the compound not so near the abbey itself. Probably a way to limit the mixing of the sacred with the profane !

Something that's good enough to be sacred, on the other hand, is the gamut of beers available, which even if they weren't or never were brewed at the abbey, each raises the bar for brewing excellence. There, and only there, visitors also have the chance to drink them from earthenware mugs.

Maredsous 10

Top fermentation – Abbey
🍺 amber
📷 Brouwerij Duvel-Moortgat, Breendonck (Anvers)
% 9,5

Tasting notes

Acidity, softness and bitterness make this clear blond with a persistent head a harmonious beer, balanced, round and full. Its nose is floral, fruity and spicy. It finishes on a note of wheat. In the mouth, it maintains its complexity and its fruitiness. It develops an after-bitterness that is agreeable, and herby aromas.

Pub secret

But what, then, is the secret to the sparkling clarity in the beers of Maredsous ? Simple : for several years, they have been filtered before being bottled to give them a superior clarity. One would think so, but as for knowing if the flavour has benefited from this operation...

Maredsous 6 Blonde

Top fermentation – Abbey
🍺 clear blond
📷 Brouwerij Duvel-Moortgat, Breendonck (Anvers)
% 6,8

Tasting notes

Maredsous Blonde presents an amber body and a creamy persistent head. In the nose, one senses lactic acid. In the mouth, it is spicy and sweet, balanced, and slightly acidic in finish.

Maredsous 6 Brune

Top fermentation – Abbey
🍺 brown
📷 Brouwerij Duvel-Moortgat, Breendonck (Anvers)
% 6,4

Tasting notes

This limpid, amber brown develops a tenacious and abundant head, as well as a significant release of gasses. To the nose, it reveals above all barley. In the mouth, · it is round, full, a little piquant and delivers barley, caramel and notes of toasted bread every time. It has a fairly dry finish.

Maredsous 8

Top fermentation – Abbey

🍺 amber brown

🏭 Brouwerij Duvel-Moortgat, Breendonck (Anvers)

% 8

Tasting notes

Brown beer with red highlights, Maredsous 8 distinguishes itself with a creamy head, slightly dark and holding well. Its release of gasses is abundant and it makes a nice effervescence. Round in the mouth, it approaches the palate well. One appreciates a pronounced flavour of roasting, followed by coffee. It finishes slightly acidic with notes of roasted almonds.

Martens (s. brewery p.132)

With a production capacity in excess of 1.000.000 hectolitres per year, installations on the cutting edge of technology and a new brewing room, the Martens brewery appears to be resolutely turned toward the future. Though this doesn't keep them from glancing into their past, because, at Martens, they carry on a tradition of 240 years, eight contiguous generations and they hold the position of oldest brewery in the province of Limbourg.

Its history begin with Adriaan Geerkens who, the 20th of March 1758, took up the café-brewing business. The site is a museum today. The first changes started around the 1860s when Franz Martens, who gave his name to the enterprise, set to brewing a

Sezoens, a beer that still exists today. The 1930s were a period of great investment in material and people, the 1950s saw the little family concern transform into an SPRL and the 80s brought them, aside from the SA status, to the state we recognize today. The brewery is also heavily involved in the preservation of the environment, and its latest installations reflect that. The most marked example being their water, pumped from a depth of 365 metres.

On the eve of the XXIst century, 80% of its production is destined for export.

Martens Pils

Bottom fermentation – Pilsner

🍺 blond

🏭 Brouwerij Martens, Bocholt (Limbourg)

% 5

The Martens brewery is number one in the Polish market for beer in cans.

Pub secret

The Martens brewery exports to several European countries, especially to the East. An exceptional fact is that it is also present in Germany, where it makes up 96% of the Belgian beer imported there. This means simply that the beer produced by the Martens brewery conforms to the famous "purity laws" of our Germanic neighbours. From the same point of view, Martens purchased a small brewery in Romania in 1998 and another in the Czech Republic (the cradle of Pilsner) in 1999 where only bottom fermented beers are brewed. This way, the enterprise has an open door to Moldavia and the Ukraine, where they also export.

Mc Chouffe

Top fermentation – Other

🍺 brown

🏭 Brasserie d'Achouffe, Achouffe (Luxembourg)

% 8,5

Tasting notes

This strong brown from the Achouffe brewery presents a nice compact head that holds well, and a significant release of gasses. The nose : above all malt accompanied by a light roasting aroma. In the mouth, it is a little dry, offering notes of liquorice as well as traces of roasting and finishing with a mixture of acidity and balanced bitterness.

🍴 roast turkey, ribs

Pub secret

They seem to like the number 6 at the Achouffe brewery, because a beer destined for the Netherlands market is marketed under the name Chouffe Bock 6666 and weighs in at 6,6%. Remember, locals as well as others, that 6666 is also the postal code for Achouffe...

Moinette *(s. brewery p.127)*

Though its name might make you think so, Moinette has no religious affiliation and therefore doesn't enter into any list of Abbey beers, official or not. This appellation is a degradation of the word *moëne* from the Tournai region's dialect, which means marsh or bog. A point of sensationalism then, since monks still don't have any female representatives among them, and even fewer wives with the title that could justify this surprising vocabulary. Even so, all this takes nothing away from the intrinsic qualities of the beers produced by Marc Rosier.

The history of one of the last farm-breweries in the country starts in 1920, when Alfred Dupont purchased the small agricultural business in order to keep his son from chasing his fortunes further afield. By the chance of an inheritance, the

Brasserie **Dupont**

Tourpes

concern became the property of the father of today's brewer, he having taken the reins in the course of the sixties. At the same time began the production of what would rapidly become the flower of the brewery : Moinette. Its available in two classic versions with the same alcohol content, one blond and one brown. Both are characterised by a cloudy appearance, thanks to re-fermentation in the bottle.

But, an itch for biological concerns drove Marc Rosier to the point when, on the eve of the 90s, he set to producing several beers meeting the strict requirements of the BIO label, from which a Moinette has today had a certain amount of success. From strictly the taste point of view, it has a lot in common with its two traditionally brewed sisters. The difference is in the regulations for hygiene during production that are followed to the letter, and an absence of pesticides and other additives that do not directly aid the culture of the hops or barley used.

Moinette Biologique

Top fermentation – Other
🍺 bright amber, slightly cloudy
🏭 Brasserie Dupont, Tourpes (Hainaut)
% 7,5

Tasting notes

The ecological Moinette dresses itself in a cloudy blond body (it isn't filtered, either), topped by a beautiful compact head that holds well. The release of gasses is about average. From an olfactory point of view, hops and wheat make up the duo of perfumes. In the mouth, it is a little acidic and piquant, offering a complex fruitiness and sprinkled with touches of malt, wheat and hops that remain well represented.
🍴 toast aux champignons, croquettes of fowl

Pub secret

Aside from the production of beer, Marc Rosier also produces bread and cheese (he kept a few cows up until April of 1999) with guaranteed quality and provenance. They are, of course, meant to be enjoyed along with the beer.

Moinette Blonde

Top fermentation – Other
🍺 bright amber, cloudy
🏭 Brasserie Dupont, Tourpes (Hainaut)
% 8,5

Tasting notes

The Moinette reveals its beautiful coppery blond body, lightly veiled (it is unfiltered), an average effervescence as well as a head that is abundant, compact and holds well. To the nose, it reveals aromas of barley, wheat and hops, accompanied by a slightly complex fruitiness. The fruitiness is found in the mouth as well, joined by notes of banana and barley as well as a prolonged, light bitterness.
🍴 lamb stew

Moinette Brune

Top fermentation – Other
🍺 deep amber, cloudy
🏭 Brasserie Dupont, Tourpes (Hainaut)
% 8,5

Tasting notes

Clear brown, the Moinette Brune develops an abundant head that holds well. To the nose, it offers aromas of barley and wheat as well as a complex fruitiness. In the mouth, it is a little piquant, presenting a balanced acidity and a nice prolonged bitterness. It is full, and distinguishes itself also with complex herby flavours.

🍴 coquilles Saint-Jacques with cream sauce

Montagnarde (La)

Top fermentation – Abbey

🍺 golden - amber

🏚 Brasserie de l'Abbaye des Rocs, Montignies sur Roc (Hainaut)

% 9

Tasting notes

Montagnarde presents a beautiful copper colour and a head that is short lived. Its acidic nose reveals aromas of caramel, barley and hops as well as an herby touch. Piquant in the mouth, it develops flavours of roasting, liquorice, and a long, persistent bitterness accompanied by a flavour of herbs and fresh hops.

Pub secret

Jean-Pierre Eloir, a federal official, was challenged one day by his father in-law, a retired brewery worker, who swore that the aforementioned was incapable of producing beer. That's how everything got started at Montignies-sur-Roc.

Mort Subite *(s. brewery p.122)*

Mort Subite (Sudden Death) – Not exactly an encouraging name to us mere mortals, huh ? But, there is nothing to fear : to our knowledge, the De Keersmaeker brewery has never poisoned anyone. The origin of the appellation is known, but we can't really keep ourselves from telling it once more. In the centre of Brussels, a café called *Brasserie Vossen* was, at noon, the rendezvous of journalists and office workers. They spent their free time drinking Gueuze and rolling dice...right up until the moment they had to return to work. So, they took up a practice called "Sudden Death", a final roll of the dice to determine a winner.

The beer they served took its name from this stage of the game and the café – that exists to this day and is still a centre of Brussels highlife – also swapped its original name for a more original moniker.

The De Keersmaeker brewery is today integrated into the Alken-Maes group, but it retains its own production unit, in Kobbegem, in Lambic's home territory. There they brew, in addition to the classic Lambic derivatives, a Gueuze infused with peach and another with blackcurrant.

Mort Subite (Framboise)

Spontaneous fermentation – Raspberry

🍺 rosé

🏚 Brouwerij De Keersmaeker, Kobbegem (Flemish Brabant)

% 4,5

Tasting notes

In its particular packaging of a corked 37,5cl bottle, the Framboise (Raspberry) offers a beautiful light head, a rosy colour and abundant bubbles. To the nose, it releases aromas of Lambic and raspberry. With an impression of acidity, it none-

Beers A to Z ◄ 89

theless develops a nice flavour of raspberry, that dissipates quickly, leaving in its place a finish composed of Lambic and a relatively pronounced flavour of artificial raspberry.

(ⵜⵜⵜ) as an aperitif, quiche Lorraine

Pub secret

The café "A la Mort Subite" or *Brasserie Vossem* (see the Belgian Beer Locator chapter), offers a menu of 50 some beers, with 11 on tap (including the Westmalle Double).

Mort Subite (Geuze)

Spontaneous fermentation – Gueuze

/🍺 coppery

🏭 Brouwerij De Keersmaeker, Kobbegem (Flemish Brabant)

% 4,5

Tasting notes

This Lambic aged in oak barrels presents a dark blond colour, slightly coppery. The bubbles are abundant, there is little head and even less bitterness. Its flavour is acidic with notes of green apple.

Mort Subite (Kriek)

Spontaneous fermentation – Kriek (Cherry)

/🍺 deep red

🏭 Brouwerij De Keersmaeker, Kobbegem (Flemish Brabant)

% 4,5

Tasting notes

Served between 8 and 9°C, Kriek (Cherry) Mort Subite presents a nice compact head, short lived,

and a strong red colour. It has a nose of Lambic, is sweet and acidic. The aromas are fairly complex, with touches of vanilla, candy almond and cherry pit. In the mouth, it is above all the cherry, Lambic and a certain acidity that compose its flavour, finishing on an acidic note. The release of gasses is substantial.

(ⵜⵜⵜ) quail with cherries

Nostradamus 9,5° (s. brewery p.124)

Top fermentation – Other

/🍺 strong brown

🏭 Brasserie Caracole, Falmignoul (Namur)

% 9,5

Tasting notes

The "Nostradamus" presents a good release of gasses. Its brown body is topped with a light head that holds well. It offers a nose of malt, accompanied by light roasting and mocha accents. Like its amber sister, it is a little piquant in the mouth and its flavour ranges among roasty, liquorice, mocha and an agreeable and pro-

Spiritualité

**Beer Brewed Carefully,
To Be Consumed With Care**

the aromas of hops (Bavarian and Yugoslavian) and wheat to bring about a beverage that broke the mould. Attentive to modern techniques, the brewery uses equipment that is relatively "state of the art", allowing them to bottle 20.000 bottles per hour. On the other hand, the label, glass and the shape of the bottle, designed by the architect Vaes, have rested more or less identical to their original versions from the thirties, which gave them their Art Deco influence. Contrary to all other Trappists, Orval is only offered in one variety. However, it holds the best promise of conservation, being allowed a minimum of 5 years to age after bottling. And it is only after a year in the bottle that it reaches its highest level of alcohol.

Often prized among connoisseurs, Orval is also one of the most appreciated beers among brewers, aside from their own, of course.

longed bitterness. In the background are notes of pear and toasted bread.

Orval (s. brewery p.132)

The founding of the Abbey goes back to the earliest days of the Middle Ages. But, with the French revolutionaries passing by, and the indelible souvenirs that they left behind, it took almost 150 years for Orval to get back on its feet. It was therefore in just 1931 that the Trappist Orval was born, created to compensate for the revenues that were generated by the forge, from back in the times of Charles Quint. This beer, of a new genre for the time (using raw hops, most notably) was put together by two lay master brewers, one Belgian and one German. They gave priority to

Orval

Top fermentation – Trappist
🍺 amber
🏠 Abbaye N.D. d'Orval (Luxembourg)
% 6,2% (7%)

Tasting notes

Coppery blond beer, with a significant release of gasses and a large head that is short lived. Its nose is fruity and acidic. As for flavour, one definitely senses the hops, with a nice prolonged bitterness, piquant, peppery and notes of pear. It is a beer with a full breadth.

Pub secret

Godefroy de Bouillon's aunt, Mathilde de Toscane, let her wedding ring fall, on purpose, into the fountain next to the abbey, in memory of her husband who died in Terre Sainte, and a trout brought the ring back to her at the surface. And so was born the legend of Val d'Or, or more poetically, Orval. One can imagine from this the symbolism that could have surrounded the recent visit from Philippe and Mathilda (of Belgium...) !

Palm *(s. brewery p.132)*

At Steenhuffel, in the Brabant, they have been brewing uninterrupted since the XVIIIth century. After the First World War, and the reconstruction that followed, Arthur Van Rooy noticed that his top fermented beer stood up well against the public mania for Pilsner. He decided then to finally give it a name "Speciale Palm" : *Speciale* for the Spéciale category of Belgian beers and *Palm*, as a sign of victory. Little by little, the successors settled in, and in 1947 a little sister was born, Dobbel, proclaiming the current mania for Christmas brews. The 1958 Expo established the notoriety of Palm, so well in fact that in 1975 the Van Rooy family, still today one of the greatest lines of independent brewers, modified the name of their brewery to match their product. In 1989 Palm struck out to conquer the export markets, especially the Netherlands and, a few years later, the global number of 30 million cases of Special has been reached.

Portrayed as the "fierté du Brabant" (Pride of the Brabant), its image as a product of quality is far ahead of its competition. Investments are made, rigorous quality control and an ecological credo are in place to support it. With their particular techniques, the brewers are equally vigilant about ensuring that the Palm in the bottle is as close as possible to the Palm from a keg. And what better represents the region than the horse of Brabant – the Belgian Draught Horse ? To establish and defend its brand image in this sense, the brewery acquired the old domain of Diepensteyn, nearby. Today we find there a stud farm as well as the National Museum of Draught Horses. A beautiful way to pay homage to those that were the heart of beer transportation.

Pater Lieven *(s. brewery p.135)*

Saint-Liévin, in Flemish Sint-Lieven, has been venerated in the region since at least the XIVth century, as testified to by a chapel built in the common of the village bearing his name. He is also the patron saint of the parish and it is well known that it is in his honour that one of the beers from the Van den Bossche brewery carries his name as well. The brewing business has been going on for more than 100 years (1897), a time when Arthur Van den Bossche bought an agricultural concern. He quickly added a brewery, the same one where still today the little family enterprise produces top fermented beers. The Pater Lieven was born one fine morning in 1957 and still rests in our time the most well known of the beers from St. Lievens Esse.

It is composed according to ancient recipes and is set down in two versions of equal alcohol, one blond and one brown. The brewery also benefits from water rich in iron, to which the villagers ascribe qualities some say are miraculous, but that have above all the ability to heal affectations of the kidneys. On the occasion of the breweries first 100 years, its patrons gave the Pater Lieven new packaging that better matched its status as a fine beer.

Pater Lieven Blond
Top fermentation – Abbey
🍷 golden blond
🏭 Brouwerij Van Den Bossche, St-Lievens Esse (East Flanders)
% 6,5

Tasting notes

This beer from the "Abbaye" category presents a golden colour and a persistent white head. It releases lightly spiced aromas of flowers and hops, coriander and citrus. Its flavour, soft and fairly neutral, reveals in its finish a nice bitterness for being fairly spicy during tasting. There are a few similarities in flavour to White Beers.

Pater Lieven Bruin
Top fermentation – Abbey
🍷 deep brown
🏭 Brouwerij Van Den Bossche, St-Lievens Esse (East Flanders)
% 6,5

Tasting notes

Dark brown sister of the Pater Lieven Blonde, it develops a nice oily head and a very fruity odour. One smells again and again perfumes of apricot, pear, peach and exotic fruits. In finish one finds aromas of malt and caramel. Its flavour is fruity, broad and full. The after-taste leaves a certain bitterness.

Pub secret

In boxes from the brewery, there also exists Lamoral Degmont. This blond, full and frank, owes its name to the Comte d'Egmont, who was suddenly separated from his head during a revolt by the Netherlands against Philippe II...

Pauwel Kwak
Top fermentation – Other
🍷 amber
🏭 Brouwerij Bosteels, Buggenhout (Flemish Brabant)
% 8

Tasting notes

Served in its traditional glass, Kwak offers a beautiful coppery colour as well as a white head, abundant and persistent. It presents a substantial release of gasses. A little piquant in the mouth, it brings up flavours of caramel, roasted malt and a light bitterness.
🍴 steak béarnaise

Pub secret

It is certain that a beer as "typée" or *individual* as this one has no lack of anecdotes, each better than the last. But the modern history of Kwak has surprised more than one drinker : as for the tasting, one must proceed with small, successive sips while the beer is in the shank of the glass. Without this, a burst of air will form and the liquid in the "balloon" at the bottom of the glass will spill out all at once. Santé !

Petrus Triple (s. brewery p.122)
Since their launch, the beers in the Petrus line have been assured of a nice little spot in the burgeoning world of Belgian

brewing. Nicknamed the "battle horse" of Bavik, Petrus Triple has been present in France since 1993, and made its entry into the Netherlands shortly thereafter.

Is this then the *Triple* that our Saint Pierre prefers ? We might imagine it, since, of the three beers that sport his name, this is the only one where he appears on the label. Maybe it is also because a *Triple* has, just by its appellation, a strong relationship with the next world... who knows ? Still, it doesn't seem to cause melancholy. Like its two eponymous sisters, it is a beer of top fermentation, individual and representative of its category. It leans strongly toward the *Spéciale*, though it is nonetheless more alcoholic (7,5% compared to the 5,5% of the *Spéciale* and the *Old Brown*).

Petrus Old Brown *(s. brewery p.122)*

This highly thirst quenching beer falls right into line with the "Browns" of its region. It ripens in oak casks for at least 24 long months, which gives it its particular character. All together, these casks total up to the tidy sum of 300.000 litres. In addition, Old Brown integrates into a triumvirate composed of beers having in common only the effigy of the pot-bellied and smiling Saint Pierre (St Petrus in Flemish), who seems to hold the keys to a paradise that we can easily imagine stocked with a few specialties from Belgium...

Petrus Triple

Top fermentation – Other
🍺 golden
📷 Brouwerij Bavik, Bavikhove (West Flanders)
% 7,5

Tasting notes

Petrus Triple presents a golden blond body, an abundant head that holds well and a significant release of gasses. It offers a very complex, floral and malty nose. In the mouth, it is full, round, well balanced and is marked by a light acidity and a prolonged bitterness, underlined by budding notes of liquorice.

🍽 beef carpaccio with truffle oil

Petrus Old Brown

Top fermentation – Flemish Brown
🍺 dark red
📷 Brouwerij Bavik, Bavikhove (West Flanders)
% 5,5

Tasting notes

This brown – as its name indicates – develops an abundant head that holds well and a significant release of gasses. In the nose, it presents a fruity and woody complexity, while in the mouth it is acidic, with accents of Port, an average fruitiness and very little bitterness. Added to this are notes of woodiness, soft caramel, chocolate, cooked pear and cinnamon. It is best appreciated when served between 9 and 13°C.

Piraat Triple IPA *(s. brewery p.137)*

Top fermentation - Special
🍺 golden amber
📷 Brouwerij Van Steenberge, Gent (East Flanders)
% 10,5

Tasting notes

Absolutely one of the top five beers of the world! A triple by strength, an IPA (Indian Pale Ale) by history. Triple means that the brewer used three times the normal amount of barley malt, starting thus with more starches, getting more sugars after cooking, and more alcohol after a long fermentation. The Piraat is re-fermented in the bottle, and in the keg! The original style of the Piraat is similar to the IPA style. It is a beer that was created many centuries ago to go on ships. Indeed, sailors drank beer on board. Nobody drank water on land, why would anybody then take water on a boat? When they started to sail out for longer voyages, the captains needed a beer with high "food" value that could be kept fresh for a long time. The Flemish sailors, called merchants by their friends and pirates by their enemies, had a very strong and potent beer like the Piraat on board.

Piraat is a wickedly rich and rounded brew that packs a mighty punch. The powerful glow builds up from inside. Deep golden with a subtle haze, it offers lots of hops and malt, with a mild sweetness. It is reminiscent of bread dough, spices and tropical fruits. Piraat goes with fish and meat. It is often appreciated as an after dinner beer, and cigar lovers claim there is no better beer to enjoy.

Poperings Hommel Ale *(s. brewery p.135)*
Top fermentation - Other
🍺 golden pale
🏭 Brouwerij Van Eecke (West Flanders)
% 7,5

Brouwerij Van Eecke

hommelbier

Tasting notes

What makes this beer special is, of course, the yeast, and what makes it unique is the higher amounts of hops used. This beer has about twice the bitterness of other Belgian beers. We can not expect less, since this beer has been brewed for centuries in the heart of the Belgian hops region: Poperinge. 'Hommel' is the local word to identify hops, and it may come from the Latin word 'humulus', used to identify hops. Some people in Poperinge believe it is the other way around: the local word was the source for the monk-scientist, many centuries ago, to create the word 'humulus'.

This is a very complex beer that you should not drink too cold, to allow the flowerly aromas and rich flavors to seduce you. The bitterness is clearly there, but is offset by a round taste of spiciness. We recommend this beer with dishes where the bitterness of the beer can offset the sweetness of the food. Depending on the sauces, white fish, chicken pastas, and game may be a good match. This beer is very refreshing and cleanses the pallet perfectly with every sip, which makes it an excellent beer to taste food.

Postel *(s. brewery p.126)*

A Norbertine abbey founded in the XIIth century, Postel, buried deep in a forest, sits at a crossroads and welcomes travellers in distress. The monks comfort their guests, according to the teachings of the founder of the order, by means of a great beer of their own making. Up until the time of the revolution when

... in short, they re-built (the buildings remained almost intact) and the abbey was occupied again in 1847, but they discontinued brewing. We must wait until the 1960s before a family brewery raised Postel back into honour. Despite its relative moderation and its absence from many bistro menus, Postel is not short on quality.

Postel Dobbel

Top fermentation – Abbey
🍺 coppery brown
🏭 Brouwerij De Smedt, Opwijk (Flemish Brabant)
% 7

Tasting notes

Limpid brown, Postel Double develops an abundant head that holds well, under which a body unfolds with red highlights and a significant release of gasses. In the nose, malt and hops dominate while in the mouth we find a nice balanced, prolonged bitterness accompanied by orange blossom. It is also round and soft.
🍽 dried figs, Postel cheese

Postel Tripel

Top fermentation – Abbey
🍺 golden blond
🏭 Brouwerij De Smedt, Opwijk (Flemish Brabant)
% 8

Tasting notes

The "Triple", a coppery blond, presents an abundant head that does not hold well and a significant release of gasses. Its principal olfactory characteristics come from malt and hops, with a fairly complex fruitiness. Round, it tastes of wheat and alcohol with similar flavour qualities as those of its sister the Double. Like the Double, this one offers a nice long bitterness.

🍴 grilled lamb

Pub secret

In the XIIth century, the founders of the Postel abbey came from the monastery at Floreffe, in the region of Namur. Today, the two communities still exist and, one can still see some points in common. One can suppose that they were both "blessed" by the care of the same architect : within the walls of each of the two groups, a modern part, somewhat "disgraceful" (to avoid calling it horrible) breaks up the unity of the original style.

Primus (s. brewery p.129)

The origins of Primus date back to the end of the XIXth century, when a dairy in Haecht profited from the popularity of bottom fermented beers by starting to sell a Pilsner. It has been some time since the dairy closed its doors, since the preparation of milk was stopped in 1929. On the other hand, Primus is still there and constitutes the fourth link in the Three Musketeers chain (Jupiler, Stella, Maes). Its name comes from Jan Primus or Jean the I[st] (Duke of Brabant from 1251 to 1294), who would become Gambrinus through successive modifications.

Eugène De Ro, the proprietor from the beginning, was really just taking up an activity that had existed at the end of the XVIth century. The Oiseau du Paradis (Bird of Paradise) was the name of this inn-brewery that had gained a reputation in the area. The enterprise became a little more perilous in 1898 for at that time there existed approximately 3223 breweries, of which 372 were in Brabant. But success was ensured, most notably, by the choice of brewing bottom fermented beers, whose popularity was just beginning and growing at the time.

Significant investment, and a direct tram line between Brussels and Haecht allowed the brewery to expand, until it reached a record number of 575.000 hl in 1937. Today's number three Pilsner brewery in Belgium launched, after the war, into a campaign of buying smaller brewing entities in Belgium and northern France.

Today, it maintains 15% of the market in the Horeca sector, supplies more than 5000 cafes across the country and has a total production of over 1.100.000 hl.

Primus Haacht

Bottom fermentation – Pilsner

🍺 pale blond

🏭 Brouwerij Haacht, Boortmeerbeek (Flemish Brabant)

% 5

Tasting notes

Primus is a golden blond offering a compact head that holds well enough and produces a significant release of gasses. In the nose, one senses above all malt. In the mouth, it makes its mark with a balanced acidity, malt again and a fine touch of hops. It has a harmonious and prolonged bitterness.

Pub secret

Up until 1975, Primus was called Super 8, an appellation with much less image. Its called "Marketing"...

Quintine *(s. brewery p.128)*

One could be a hermit where beer is concerned, and still be aware of Quintine. Its bottle, bestowed with a crockery cork and a rubber ring – typical of olden times – is a common sight and inevitably symbolises the spirit. The region of origin for this bitter blond is also "responsible" for the notoriety of Quintine. Down there, the local folklore is full of tales of sorcerers, and it is one of these, a benevolent one, that gives its name to this beer from Ellezelles. Quintine first emerged in 1993, thanks to the cares of Philippe Gérard for whom brewing skills were no fairy tale since he had previously worked at Dubuisson.

Quintine

Top fermentation – Other

🍺 blond

🏭 Brasserie Ellezelloise, Ellezelles (Hainaut)

% 8

Tasting notes

Nicknamed "bière des Collines" (beer of the hills), Quintine is re-fermented in the bottle. A dark blond colour, it develops a small head and not much gas is released. It is also slightly cloudy. It has a nice nose of barley, a nice balance of body and prolonged finish of malted barley. Also noticeable is a lingering in the mouth and a convincing bitterness.

🍽 pheasant, red meat, cold cuts, sausages and pates, hard rind cheeses, fresh goat cheese

Rochefort *(s. brewery p.121)*

Contrary to the other two Trappist abbeys in the Walloon region, the monks of Rochefort do not make cheese, even though many people think they do. Yielding no doubt to the pressure, a "lay" cheese, essentially aimed at the tourist market has appeared to support the beer.

Here though, the monks make only beer, available in three versions each more admirable than the last. In this monastery dedicated to Saint Rémy, many times destroyed and re-built with the same ardour, the walls sheltered, up until the XVth century ... cloisters. However, their task becoming too arduous no doubt, they ceded their abbey to monks, who brought to Rochefort an ever-growing reputation. Far from all the hustle and bustle of modern life, the religious have executed their brewing skills since that time, with almost no major modifications. The production has remained fairly low (15.000 hectolitres per year) and access to the Cistercian site, though reportedly of immeasurable beauty (in a valley where a tributary of the Lhomme flows) is still tantamount to mounting an attack for a common layperson to gain access.

Rochefort 6

Top fermentation – Trappist
🍺 amber
🏚 Abbaye N.D. St Rémy, Rochefort (Namur)
% 7,5

Tasting notes

This Trappist presents a lightly veiled brown body, abundant effervescence and a significant, compact head that holds well. In the nose, one picks up mostly notes of malt and pear. In the mouth, it is a little acidic but also recalls its olfactory characteristics, along with the addition of mocha, liquorice and a light bitterness.

Rochefort 8

Top fermentation – Trappist
🍺 brown
🏚 Abbaye N.D. St Rémy, Rochefort (Namur)
% 9,5

Tasting notes

"8" is a lightly veiled brown, with a head that is short lived and a significant release of gasses. Fruity to the nose, it also presents a light roasting smell. In the mouth, it is full, light, offering a balanced bitterness, notes of banana and pear, anis and liquorice.
(🍴) saddle of hare, veal liver

Rochefort 10

Top fermentation – Trappist
🍺 dark brown
🏚 Abbaye N.D. St Rémy, Rochefort (Namur)
% 11,3

Tasting notes

The Rochefort 10 is a very dark brown beer, with abundant bubbles and a head that doesn't hold well. It presents a nose of barley, caramel and roasting aromas. In the mouth, it offers a bitter lingering, with notes of apple and chocolate.

Pub secret

A few years ago a Greek friend of the Petit Futé, having lived in Belgium for three years, began his exploration of Belgian beers with a Rochefort 10... A very memorable phrase was born of that encounter : "Rochefort, c'est fort!!" ("Rochefort, it *is* strong!!")

Rodenbach *(s. brewery p.132)*

Absorbed in 1998 by Palm, Rodenbach was up until then a small family brewery. The founders, four brothers in 1820, were the descendants of a German knight who settled in Roulers in the XVIIIth century. They also had lines of parentage in common with the poet Georges Rodenbach. Two generations later, Eugène Rodenbach brought back from England the secrets of aging in oak barrels, which resulted in the very individual beer that we know today. The making of Rodenbach still goes back to its ancient traditions : some of the oak casks are 150 years old and reeds are still used to keep the huge 650 hl barrels watertight. The beer also takes its own sweet time to age : it makes us wait at least 20 months before being consumed. As for its inimitable flavour, it comes from this barrel aging and its wheat, which is the same as that used in its beginnings.

Well appreciated abroad, it was with a platinum medal that the Rodenbach Alexander returned from World Championships in 1998. As for a difference between the two sisters of the brewery, this one is made with cherries, though completely different from the Krieks of the Brussels region. Its production will unfortunately be halted this year, but since this brew demands a two year aging period in the cave, it will still be available for the next few months.

Rodenbach Alexander

Top fermentation – Flemish Brown

🍺 brown - red

🏭 Brouwerij Rodenbach, Roeselare (West Flanders)

% 6

Tasting notes

The Alexander presents a clear brown body, a weak head that is short lived and a significant release of gasses. The nose is fruity, woody, soft and sugary. We find the same softness in the mouth, accompanied by a certain acidity and a perfume of cherry. It leaves notes of passion fruit and a weak bitterness.

Pub secret

In Belgium, 2,767 families live on a street, or avenue, or place named... "Rodenbach". A chance for the brewery, last year, to launch an excellent promotion : messengers, sent by Rodenbach took advantage of the new look of their brand to offer four bottles of their beer to the people that lived at these addresses.

Since they have promised to do this again, see if maybe you can move...

Rodenbach Grand Cru

Top fermentation – Flemish Brown

🍺 brown - red

🏭 Brouwerij Rodenbach, Roeselare (West Flanders)

% 6

Tasting notes

The "Grand Cru" offers the eye a pretty brown body with red highlights and a nice head, compact and holding well. It presents a significant release of gasses and a weak bitterness. In the mouth, it develops nuances of vanilla, a taste of passion fruit and a fresh and lively acidity.

🍽 peel-and-eat shrimp

Rodenbach

Top fermentation – Flemish Brown

🍺 brown - red

🏭 Brouwerij Rodenbach, Roeselare (West Flanders)

% 5

Tasting notes

A beer of mixed fermentation (top and spontaneous), brown and aged in oak barrels for two years. The head is short lived, the nose is fresh and fruity. It presents a neat acidity that is prolonged in a roasting flavour, joined by a note of passion fruit, iron and oak. The finish is a little bitter and piquant.

Roman *(s. brewery p.133)*

The Roman brewery is a unique case in Belgian brewing : it can take pride in a beautiful continuity. Founded in 1545, it is directed today by L.-C. Roman, twelfth generation of the direct family line. In its origin, between Cologne and Dunkerque there was found an inn called "De Clocke". This was a relay point for horses and also housed a brewery. More than 450 years later, the inn of the early days has disappeared but the family spirit remains and has made room for modern facilities. Situated near the village of Audenarde, in the heart of the region nicknamed the "Flemish Ardennes", the brewery was able to preserve its independence in the face of the "giant" Belgian Pilsner manufacturers, against whom they compete with an array of more unique beers.

Romy Pils
Bottom fermentation – Pilsner
🍺 golden blond
🏭 Brouwerij Roman, Mater (East Flanders)
% 5,1

Tasting notes
This golden blond offers a significant release of gasses and a light head that disappears quickly. It releases a malty, fruity aroma, with notes of honey. Soft and round in the mouth, it develops a light acidity. The hops is well represented as is the malt. One tastes a certain bitterness, late and balanced.
🍴 tapenade with nuts

Rosé de Gambrinus
Spontaneous fermentation – Kriek (Cherry)
🍺 red, rosé
🏭 Brasserie Cantillon, Anderlecht (Bruxelles)
% 5

Tasting notes
To the nose, the "Rosé" presents a bouquet of young Lambic, waves of cherry and raspberry. It is a little winy. Very acidic in the mouth, one remarks on a nice prolonged bitterness.

Pub secret
While visiting the Cantillon brewery, you can learn that the brewers of Lambic are and remain very respectful of the environment that surrounds them. A few examples ? Regular shipments of fresh fruits inevitably attract insects, that themselves invite spiders. These are the guarantors of biological equilibrium in the brewery, destroying a large number of parasites on the brewing activities. Numerous spider webs decorate the corners of the brewery buildings, and no brewer knocks them down. In fact, to that same end, when a repair to the roof was required, the old tiles were left in place under the new tiles in order not to disturb the biological equilibrium in the room.

Saint-Louis
(s. brewery p.137)
Even though Lambic is principally produced in the valley of the Senne on the Brussels periphery, everything points to there being a micro-region around Kortrijk (Courtrai) that benefits from the same bacteriological characteristics, because we find beers there that assert their membership in the Lambic family. Which brings to mind an old adage about the exception confirming the rule !

That being said, the Saint Louis line has existed for many years, and no one seems to be upset by them.

Its history began in Ingelmunster in 1900, exactly 100 years ago, when the Van Honsbrouck newlyweds bought a farm and founded a brewery. Their sons Paul and Ernest kept it going in 1922. The enterprise took a decidedly professional turn when Luc Van Honsbrouck, son and nephew of the above, studied brewing science. He took over direction of operations in 1953 and is still today at the head of the brewery. He added his letters of nobility to Saint Louis, while leading it down a path with a long series of fruit versions and giving birth to the other best-sellers of the brewery : the *Brigand* and the *Kasteelbier*.

Expanding its presence on the export market, the Van Honsebrouck brewery markets its products in all neighbouring countries (except Luxembourg), Finland, Spain, Italy, North America and Japan.

Saint-Louis (Framboise)

Spontaneous fermentation – Framboise (Raspberry)

🍺 sombre red

📷 Brouwerij Van Honsebrouck, Ingelmunster (West Flanders)

% 4,5

Tasting notes

Its pink head of foam tops a mahogany brown body. One discovers complex aromas of raspberry, a little cherry, a certain acidity and a few notes of nuttiness. Fairly sweet in taste, it offers nonetheless a nicely built acidity.

Pub secret

Saint-Louis (Geuze Lambic)

Spontaneous fermentation – Gueuze

🍺 golden

📷 Brouwerij Van Honsebrouck, Ingelmunster (West Flanders)

% 5

Tasting notes

The gueuze from Ingelmunster presents a golden blond body, an abundant head that is short lived and an average effervescence. It is soft in the nose and offers olfactory sensations of Lambic, nuts, almond, apple and syrup. One finds the same sensations in the mouth, accompanied by a small bitterness and a medicinal aftertaste.

Saint-Louis (Kriek)

Spontaneous fermentation – Kriek (Cherry)

🍺 mahogany

📷 Brouwerij Van Honsebrouck, Ingelmunster (West Flanders)

% 4,5

Tasting notes

The Saint Louis Kriek presents, under a bright head, a mahogany brown body. Fairly complex in the nose, it offers aromas of wood, cherries, nuts and candy. In the mouth one notes a fresh acidity, little fruit, a lack of roundness and a light post-bitterness with notes of caramel making up the aftertaste.

Sara Buckwheat Ale *(s. brewery p.133)*

Top fermentation - Other

🍺 brown red

📷 Brasserie De Silenrieux (Province of Namur)

Brasserie Silenrieux

Organic

Sara Buckwheat Ale
Joseph Spelt Ale

Imported by Win-It-Too Inc. • P.O. Box 2069 • Santa Barbara CA 93120 • Tel. 1-800-442-3379

% 6

Tasting notes

The organic beer Sara has a red-brown color, is well hopped and spicy at the same time, and comes with a dense head. It has a hearty, exclusively special, refreshing taste that stays behind in your throat. Some of us find faint sour undertones, but these are certainly not dominant. The aroma is specific and unique, something you may expect since you've probably never had a buckwheat beer before. Buckwheat is also known as 'black grain' and is a very round small ball-shaped grain, black on the outside but white inside. It is an easy growing simple grain, very rich with starches. The buckwheat is not malted, but milled before it enters the mash-tun. Not more than 25 % of Buckwheat is used, the rest is barley malt. Buckwheat has been raised for centuries on the farms of Silenrieux, and it is not a surprise that the locals used it to brew their beers. We recommend Sara as a heart warming beer in the evening. It goes very well with meat dishes. There is an adventurous flavor in the beer to be offset or augmented by the spices in the food. An excellent beer to marinate.

Satan *(s. brewery p.126)*

What could be more normal that to find a beer named simply "Red Devil" in Belgium... It makes sense and its surprising that no one thought of it before, even though this has been a part of the brewing landscape for a dozen years already. The De Block brewery, one of the last family breweries in the region, born in 1887, has shown the way. They offer a beer for which, they maintain, a geographical proximity to the Lambic region is probably not innocent in the fruity taste that it frankly announces. So here then is a great beer, from the midst of a region plentiful in renowned breweries. It should be noted that there is another version, this one a blond, from Satan. It is named Gold, presents similar characteristics of taste and is less widely distributed.

But what really strikes one on visiting the brewery is the familial and convivial atmosphere, reinforced by the bells of the neighbouring church that "sing" every quarter hour. A bistro, just as charming, set up in the old byre, completes the scene of rustic ambiance. Today, the production floats between 6 and 8 thousand hectolitres annually and the beers of the De Bloch brewery (Satan Red and Gold, to which they agreeably added the Triple Dendermonde, which appeared three years ago) are exported everywhere, from Canada to Japan, by way of Europe.

Satan Gold

Top fermentation – Other

🍺 russet yellow

🏭 Brouwerij De Block, Merchtem-Peizegem (Flemish Brabant)

% 8

Tasting notes

Re-fermented in the bottle, Satan Gold presents a pleasant coppery blond colour and an abundant release of gasses. It develops a nice white head that holds well. In the nose, there is

principally barley and wheat. Round and full in the mouth, it reveals well presented flavours of hops, herby notes as well as a pronounced, well balanced bitterness.

Satan Red

Top fermentation – Other

🍺 amber - copper

🏭 Brouwerij De Block, Merchtem-Peizegem (Flemish Brabant)

% 8

Tasting notes

The amber Satan develops a compact and tenacious head, accompanied by a significant release of gasses. It reveals in its nose a complex of fruit and acidity, strengthened by aromas of barley and wheat. In the mouth, it is a little piquant, barley and wheat being very present. One also senses a light roasting and a weak bitterness that is fairly short.

🍽 guinea fowl, pheasant

Pub secret

In Paris, the city of light, capital of the universe, six cafes serve Satan on tap. A bit of information to cheer expatriate amateurs in France as well as our cousins from Outre-Quiévrain, even though a beer is always better enjoyed when drunk in its land of origin...

Saxo

Top fermentation – Other

🍺 blond

🏭 Brasserie Caracole, Falmignoul (Namur)

% 7,2

Tasting notes

Here is a golden blond that develops a nice compact head that holds well. Its release of gasses is significant. In the nose, we sense barley and wheat as well as an agreeable touch of malt. It is a little piquant in the mouth, offering a light flavour of roasting and revealing the presence of hops. It has a characteristic bitterness that is prolonged and balanced with complex notes of fruit.

🍴 grilled lobster

Scotch de Silly *(s. brewery p.133)*

Top fermentation - Other
🍺 dark red
🏭 Brasserie de Silly, Silly (Hainaut)
% 8

Tasting notes

This hearty Scotch ale offers a smooth, really velvety taste with a "hoppy" bitterness. Some licorice undertones is what you expect and find in a real Scotch ale. It is brewed with pure malts, English hops and some candy sugars during the fermentation process. Why does Silly brew a Scottish beer? Well, a Scottish regiment of the British army was based in the village of Silly right after WW I. The only beverage an army could safely rely on in that era was beer. So, the Captains of that Scottish Regiment asked the local brewery to brew a beer that was to the liking of the Scottish soldiers. It is not clear if the brew recipe was also given to the brewery by the Captains, or if the brewery created this exceptional beer on its own. The fact is that the British army supplied the English hops, since Poperinge, the main source in Belgium for hops, was completely destroyed during the war.

Sloeber *(s. brewery p.133)*

The least we can write is that Sloeber isn't particularly well known outside of its home region, an area particularly favoured by professional cyclists. This soft amber, steeped in the tradition of its genre, is in effect nowhere to be found outside of the cafes stamped "Roman" and in specialist houses. Strange to be so discrete and yet so politically correct, since in Vondel's language, its name means mischievous, scamp...

Sloeber

Top fermentation – Other
🍺 amber
🏭 Brouwerij Roman, Mater (East Flanders)
% 7,5

Tasting notes

This discrete coppery blond develops an abundant head that holds well and a generous effervescence. It is supple and mellow. It offers a nose that is malty and aromatic, followed by a dry finish of orange zest. It is best served at 10°C.

🍴 terrines, pigs feet

Speciale Palm

Top fermentation – Ale
🍺 amber
🏭 Brouwerij Palm, Steenhuffel (Flemish Brabant)
% 5,1

Tasting notes

Palm develops an abundant head that holds well. It has a significant release of gasses. Best served at 12°C, it offers a nice strong bitterness. It leaves a finish that is round, with nuances of orange and wheat.

🍴 mussel casserole

Pub secret

Available in the Netherlands since 1989, Palm has only enlarged its penetration and reached, in 1998, 25% of the market for special beers with our neighbours to the north. This progress by the brewery merited its reception, the 6th of September 1999, of the Pépite (or Sabot) d'Or, a distinction to reward the Belgian or Dutch enterprise with the greatest increase in Dutch market share over the preceding year. The trophy was given to the prize-winners by Jean-Luc Dehaene, past Prime Minister,... and inveterate beer drinker!!

St Bernardus
(s. brewery p.134)

Many abbey beers are lumped together by neophytes with their Trappist sister brews and generally, this is an error, even if the abbey brew is also moulded with the same real qualities. But in the present case, the confusion is justified, and a good number of amateurs will admit that they were once taken in by this one. It is true that there is plenty here to lead one astray. Judge for yourself : St Bernardus used to be called St Sixtus and was brewed in a brewery situated on ... *Trappistenweg* (Trappist Road) in Watou. Not for from

there, we find the St Sixtus abbey ... brewing their own beer, the famous Westvleteren of which there is a lot of talk but rare occasion to taste. The present confusion also springs from the fact that the religious community authorised this brewer to market its product under their name, from 1946 until 1992. Are you with me so far ? All this has been put back into order (pardon the pun) recently, with the abbey taking back the rights to its appellation...

That being said, the St Bernardus(es) might have merited the term "Trappist", just by their numerous similarities and their incontestable quality.

St Bernardus Abt12
Top fermentation – Abbey

🍺 dark amber

🏭 Brouwerij St Bernardus, Watou (West Flanders)

% 10

Tasting notes

"Abt" is a dark beer, developing an abundant light brown head that holds well and presents a significant release of gasses. In the nose, it delivers aromas of pears and a roasting scent that doesn't force its dominance. Full in the mouth, it adds to the perfumes already listed flavours of liquorice and a light, somewhat winy bitterness.

🍴 veal knuckle

St Bernardus Pater 6
Top fermentation – Abbey

🍺 brown

🏭 Brouwerij St Bernardus, Watou (West Flanders)

% 6,7

Tasting notes

The St Bernardus Pater presents a bright brown body, an abundant head that holds well, and a significant effervescence. Under its nose of barley, one senses a light roasting and notes of liquorice and caramel. The same characteristics are found again in the mouth, underlined with pear and mocha. There is an appreciable, light, prolonged bitterness as well.

(🍴) hard rind cheese, croquettes of fowl

St Bernardus Prior 8

Top fermentation – Abbey

🍺 amber

🏭 Brouwerij St Bernardus, Watou (West Flanders)

% 8

Tasting notes

The St Bernardus Prior is a strong brown, characterised by a significant release of gasses, and an abundant head that holds poorly. To the nose, it is soft, fruity, malty. In the mouth, it is a little piquant and reveals perfumes of roasting, banana, liquorice, and a light, prolonged bitterness.

(🍴) leg of lamb

St Bernardus Triple

Top fermentation – Abbey

🍺 golden

🏭 Brouwerij St Bernardus, Watou (West Flanders)

% 7,5

Tasting notes

Its bright blond body and persistent head reveal a beer that is balanced and complex, with aromas of pear, banana and crème fraîche. One finds the same harmonious complexity in the mouth, in conjunction with notes of peach and honey.

Pub secret

To further the mystery along, this brewery is called St Bernardus (remember, the founder of the Cistercian order was Saint Bernardus) and it continues to brew nothing but this one beer, the same as the Trappists, who produce just their one brew. Therefore, there is no direct link to the other breweries in the area who, to top it all off, also produce abbey beers.

St Feuillien
(s. brewery p.129)

Feuillien arrived from Ireland, in the VIIth century, to Evangelise. One day in the year 655, while he was passing through the forest at Roeulx (Hainaut), he was tortured and decapitated. His followers erected a chapel there, and in 1125 an abbey of Prémontrés was established. The monks brewed a beer there, as was the habit of most of these communities. Then, the Revolution... In 1873, the Friart family, installed in Roeulx, took up the ancestral recipe and, supplied with water from a gushing spring under the brewery, breathed "life" back into St Feuillien.

Since 1920, more modern buildings house the facilities still in use today. The fifties marked the apogee of the brewery since it was then that they produced a wide range of beers (including a Pilsner) in addition to St Feuillien. In 1980, after having already abandoned all its other beers, the Friart brewery, unable to continue under its extended investments, confided the production to the du Bocq brewery and closed its doors. The brewery in Namur set about producing St Feuillien, in bottles of 25 and 75 cl.

But, this was without counting on the energy of Benoît Friart the third, and of his sister. The fermentation vats had barely cooled when in 1986 they decided to refurbish the facilities in Roeulx and to rack the beer in magnums. And, in 1988, the brewery re-launched its activities.

The beacon product is the St Feuillien Blonde, a beer of character, that spends six weeks at 0°C to allow its flavour to refine itself, before a three week sojourn at 25°C. And that is how St Feuillien is born...

St Feuillien Blonde

Top fermentation – Abbey

🍺 golden blond, lightly clouded

📷 Brasserie Friart, Le Roeulx (Hainaut), Brasserie du Bocq (Namur)

% 7,5

Tasting notes

Of a golden blond colour, slightly cloudy, St Feuillien develops a very dense and persistent head. Its approach is lively, a little acidic with drier nuances that follow. The hops is very present and the aromas are complex (juniper berry, coriander, lime, citrus, celery, ...). Served at 6°C as an aperitif and 12°C during the meal.

St Feuillien Brune

Top fermentation – Abbey

🍺 fawn brown

📷 Brasserie Friart, Le Roeulx (Hainaut), Brasserie du Bocq (Namur)

% 7,5

Tasting notes

St Feuillien Brune is a limpid beer, developing an abundant head that holds well, and with a significant release of gasses. It reveals aromas of malt, caramel and mocha, while hops is also present. A little piquant in the mouth, it leaves flavours of roasting and mocha, accompanied by points of liquorice and pear.

🍴 grilled steak, guinea fowl

Pub secret

St Feuillien is brewed half (magnums, jéroboams, ...) in Roeulx (at the Friart Brewery) and the other half at the du Bocq Brewery. That's one way to keep peace between the creator of the brew, and those who kept it alive during the lean years.

St Paul (s. brewery p.135)

We are not entirely sure how things got started at the Sterkens brewery and, evidently, the current proprietors, Fons and Stan, aren't any better informed. The oldest documentation is a notarised act from 1731, showing that there was already brewing activity at the time. However, it is impossible to find other evidence from earlier times. As for events since then, we can definitely attest to the fact that an agricultural pursuit existed for dozens of years right alongside the brewing. This practice being, as we have seen, very common at the time.

St Paul is available in many variations of a common theme : blond, double, triple or special and dresses itself in a beautiful and unique bottle. Concurrently, the Sterkens brewery lays claim to the paternity of a *St Sebastiaan*, also packaged in a unique manner, and a *Bokrijks Kruikenbier*.

The products of the Sterkens brewery are found in most nearby countries, and also in the United States, South Africa, Japan and New Zealand.

St Paul Double

Top fermentation – Abbey

🍺 mahogany

🏭 Brouwerij Sterkens, Hoogstraten (Anvers)

% 6,9

Tasting notes

The St Paul Double is a brown with red highlights, presenting a weak head that is short lived and an average release of gasses. In the nose, it develops aromas of mocha, liquorice and a light roasting. In the mouth, it is soft, sweet, fruity, a little piquant. One also finds a light roasting flavour and a weak and short bitterness.

St Paul Triple

Top fermentation – Abbey

🍺 golden blond

🏭 Brouwerij Sterkens, Hoogstraten (Anvers)

% 7,6

Tasting notes

The Triple reveals a blond body, almost amber, very strong and not cloudy. Its head is light and holds poorly while its release of

gasses is about average. After a nose of malt and hops, it is slightly piquant in the mouth, distilling a certain bitterness. Barley has a strong presence as well.

Steendonck
(s. brewery p.132)

Contrary to what one might think, competitors are not necessarily enemies... The best proof of that is probably this White Beer, the fruit of an association between two large independent breweries, Palm and Duvel-Moortgat. The result of their relationship is Steendonck, whose name comes from a simple contraction of Steenhuffel and Breendonck, the original sites of each of its "parents". Its apparition was due more to the desire to combat the relative hegemony of Hoegaarden rather than to try and occupy the niche for White Beers that are more special or authentic.

Steendonck

Top fermentation – White Beer

🍺 pale yellow, cloudy

🏭 Brouwerij Palm, Steenhuffel (Flemish Brabant)

% 4,5

Tasting notes

A beer with a cloudy blond body, its white head does not last long. It develops a nose of wheat, citrus and coriander and offers little body. In the mouth, it presents a fresh flavour, citric with a note of coriander and very little bitterness. Thirst quenching, it distinguishes itself with a complex character, terminating in an herby finish that brings to mind bay laurel.

Stella Artois
(s. brewery p.130)

The city of Leuven and the brewery have been intimately linked for generations ; documents dating from 1366 attest to transactions between the authorities and the inn-brewery Den Hoorn. The year 1708 was also decisive : it was then that Sébastien Artois was given the title of Master-Brewer at Den Hoorn. Stella, the beer of a country of beer, became an integral part of the Belgian brewing world in 1926, at the time when Pilsner first appeared. From that moment, it has never left the forefront of the scene, and remains to this day the number two Belgian, just behind its cousin from the Cité Ardente. It is also associated with everyday beer drinking. And, for special occasions, Interbrew has taken care of everything, since Stella is now available in a "duotank" of 200 litres, delivered directly by refrigerated truck.

In other news, the Interbrew group has seen a very lively year 2000. To whit, after announcing its entry on the Bourse, slated for the end of December, it did a little shopping on the English market. Into its basket, Interbrew – who employs some 24.000 people worldwide – put the British brewer Whitbread, purchased for the modest sum of 26,6 billion Belgian francs, or 400.000.000 £. At the same time, the Belgian group took back control of Stella Artois, brewed in Great Britain by Whitbread since 1976.

But the Louven based company didn't stop there, since we have learned in the fall-out that the parents of the twins Stella and Jupiler are uniting with the Bass group, the price being fixed at 140 billion Belgian francs. Interbrew will henceforth occupy the number two position in the world's Top market sectors and will situate itself on the upper echelon in Europe.

Stella Artois

Bottom fermentation – Pilsner

🍺 blond

🏭 Brouwerij Interbrew, Leuven (Flemish Brabant)

% 5,2

Tasting notes

Stella, under a beautiful white head that is light and holds well, presents a pleasant golden blond colour, a weak effervescence and a nose of slightly piquant barley. Short in the mouth, it offers a light bitterness, accompanied by herby touches. It is a fresh and thirst quenching beer.

Pub secret

Stella, from the Artois brewery, was originally brewed specially for Christmas 1926, something that is still done today in quite a few places. It owes its name to its particularly light colour, shiny like a star (*étoile* in French), and its perennial presence due to its immediate popularity. It is an interesting detail to this story, bearing witness to changing tastes and habits, that Christmas beers today are generally high in alcohol and a strong, dark colour.

Stella Artois N.A. (Non Alcohol)

Bottom fermentation – N.A.

🍺 golden blond

📷 Brouwerij Interbrew, Leuven (Flemish Brabant)

% max. 0,5

Tasting notes

Stella N.A. is a coppery blond, that develops an abundant head that is short lived. There is a significant release of gasses. The nose develops pronounced scents of grains and notes of honey. Short in the mouth, it presents little bitterness and fairly pronounced honey elements.

Super des Fagnes
(s. brewery p.128)

The Fagnes brewery opened its doors in April 1998 and then brewed 375 hectolitres annually. This number has been constantly growing. Specialising in making craft beers, of which the famous "Super des Fagnes" is one, they recently formulated a plan to attract visitors, and thereby blend technology and tourism.

With four 1400 litre vats and one 700 litre vat at their disposal, they are able to make beers of top or bottom fermentation, beers brewed with nitrogen (like Guiness) and fruit beers as well as aperitifs and soft drinks. The brews for tasting in the brewery come straight from the vats. The beers change regularly, with the seasons, bringing the smells and feelings of nature. The Fagnes brewery also brings back beers that have "disappeared" by finding old recipes and interviewing old brewers. An excellent way to create a tie

with the "museum" brewery, dating from 1858.

But the flower of Frédéric Adant and his team is recognized as the famous "Super". A veritable icon in its region, and even though it is a relatively recent conception, it extends its territory a little more each day, and has expanded outside the boundaries of Fagnes in Namur. Even so, sales and location still have a mostly local character. One notable exception : it is distributed in the 7 Cora stores throughout the country. As for the product itself, its main characteristic is its non-pasteurisation, thanks to which its flavour evolves over time.

Super des Fagnes

Top fermentation – Other

🍺 blond

📷 Brasserie des Fagnes, Couvin (Namur)

% 7,7

Tasting notes

A "Super" is best served between 6 and 10°C. It develops a very beautiful head that holds well. Its body is blond, very slightly clouded, and gives an abundant release of gasses. It reveals an herby and complex nose. Fairly acidic in the mouth, it brings up malt, wheat and hops flavours. In its finish, one receives a nice balanced bitterness and traces of biscuit.

🍴 codfish with cream sauce *mousseline*

Pub secret

If you have the desire to drink a beer that is made exactly to your tastes, then know that the Fagnes brewery can fill that bill for you. They also brew "ponctuelle" ("daily", or "of the hour") beers : ancient recipes, nettle beers and other experiments. And during your visit, you can't miss the tasting menu for any reason... it allows the tasting of four (small) different glasses accompanied by cheese.

Timmermans *(s. brewery p.135)*

From the European Capital you could throw a head of hops and hit... the Timmermans brewery, taken over in 1993 by the John Martin group, which produces traditional Lambics. Here we find the classic Gueuze, a Kriek with real mashed Schaerbeek cherries, a raspberry made according to the same model, a peach Lambic and a Faro. Aside from this regular array, Timmermans offers a "Blanche (White) Lambic", a spontaneously fermented beer made according to the method prescribed for White Beers.

Timmermans Framboise

Spontaneous fermentation – Raspberry

deep red

Brouwerij Timmermans, Itterbeek (Flemish Brabant)

% 5

Tasting notes

A red body and a pink head make up its look. It develops an acidic and sugary scent, a touch of cooked vegetable, wood and above all raspberry. In the mouth, it is acid, sweet, tannic and lacks a little bite.

Timmermans Gueuze Caveau

Spontaneous fermentation – Gueuze

golden amber

Brouwerij Timmermans, Itterbeek (Flemish Brabant)

% 5,5

Tasting notes

This is a coppery blond, lightly clouded, presenting a considerable release of gasses and an abundant head that is short lived. In the nose, one can easily discern Lambic, woody notes, a complex fruitiness and accents of green apple. In the mouth, it is full, round, and offers a balanced acidity with charateristics similar to its nose. It also lingers in the mouth.

Timmermans Kriek

Spontaneous fermentation – Kriek (Cherry)

red

Brouwerij Timmermans, Itterbeek (Flemish Brabant)

% 5

Tasting notes

A bright red colour with its slightly pink head, it presents the typical Kriek taste, that is : nuts, wood, acidity and cooked vegetables. It is sweet enough in the mouth then develops a pronounced acidity while the cherries are well presented. It should be served in the neighbourhood of 8-9°C.

Tongerlo *(s. brewery p.129)*

The Tongerlo abbey dates from the XIIth century (between 1130 and 1133) and, after having survived the ages without too much damage, suffered the horrors of the Revolution, sale for the notional benefit in 1839 and finally a fire in 1929. We can well understand from this why the Norbertine monks (responding then to the same rules as Leffe, Grimbergen or Postel) might no longer want to continue an activity that was nonetheless beloved, and confided their recipes to the brewers at Haacht, who re-launched the brand on the market in 1990. The traditional Double and Triple saw the birth of, a few years after their own "re-birth", a little sister to complete the family.

The peculiarity of the "Double Blond" isn't just its colour, frankly rather light for a *Double*, but above all the fact that it is built as a veritable union between the *Double* and *Triple* : it has characteristics that one would imagine from a fusion of the two types, to such a degree in fact that it appears to be the legitimate progeny of its two "progenitors".

Among others, it belongs to the famous category of "Beers from Well-Known Abbeys".

On the ecclesiastical side, the abbey is famous for its copy of a work by Leonardo de Vinci (la *Cène*), executed during the artist's life for the abbey itself. It is still open for public access.

Tongerlo Dubbel Blond

Top fermentation – Abbey

🍺 coppery blond

📷 Brouwerij Haacht (Flemish Brabant)

% 6

Tasting notes

The Double Blonde from Tongerlo offers a beautiful amber colour, and a head that is abundant and holds well. Its nose gives hints of Madeira, malt and caramel. Its flavour is

malty and oxidised to such a point that the finish in the mouth is somewhat dry.

Pub secret

The Haacht brewery shows a great deal of respect for the environment. To whit, a complete wastewater purification station has been installed there. Working in a biological manner, this station actually serves to improve the quality of the Leibeek waters, a river that runs nearby. As for the residual sludge, it is used by the farmers in the area to amend their soil.

According to the same ideals, the brewery has used, since 1988, cadmium free racks and recyclable glassware for its public celebrations.

Tongerlo Dubbel

Top fermentation – Abbey

🍺 translucent brown

📷 Brouwerij Haacht (Flemish Brabant)

% 6

Tasting notes

An abundant head that holds well tops the beautiful brown body of the Tongerlo brew. In the nose, it reveals scents of barley and caramel. In the mouth, it is round, alcoholic (a little winy) and presents a light roasting. One gets flavours of liquorice, anis and chocolate, deepened by a balanced bitterness.

🍴 grilled red meats

Tongerlo Tripel

Top fermentation – Abbey

🍺 blond

📷 Brouwerij Haacht (Flemish Brabant)

% 8

The Triple presents a light blond body and a persistent head. It is relatively acidic and spicy and one notices particularly aromas of coriander and grapefruit. Its hoppy taste is strongly spiced, underlined by a marked bitterness, in concert with a significant release of gasses. Slightly piquant in the mouth, it develops some flavour of roasting, a strong stamp of alcohol as well as a complex, herby touch with notes of bay laurel.

Triple Karmeliet *(s. brewery p.123)*

The youngest issue from the Bosteels brewery strictly applies the rule of threes : triple fermentation, a density equal to an abbey Triple and the use of three grains (wheat, barley and oats). Pulled from the files of Antoine Bosteels, today's seventh generation leader, the Triple was conceived according to the principles used today for multi-grain breads. A little help from a fairy godmother and the breweries total production surpasses 24.000 hectolitres, a very tidy amount for a little family business. But, luck has been no stranger to the success of the Triple : in the XVIIth century, a convent in Dendermonde (Termonde) produced a beer with very similar characteristics. Antoine Bosteels jumped on the chance to make use of this and gave his new creation a slightly religious character...

Triple Karmeliet

Top fermentation – Other

🍺 golden blond

📷 Brouwerij Bosteels, Buggenhout (Flemish Brabant)

% 8

The Triple Karmeliet is characterised by a golden colour, slightly orange, a white, creamy and abundant head with aromas of vanilla and orange, wheat and citrus. In the nose, one discerns citrus fruit and coriander. In the mouth, the approach is soft, and the aromas complex, dominated by fruity flavours.

🍴 Red meats, Herve cheese.

Pub secret

The success of the Triple Karmeliet was huge : M. Jackson was, to say the least, laudatory on the subject, it received several gold medals at international competitions and one restaurant, rated by the *maison Bibendum*, (Karmeliet!!) recently included the Triple on its menu.

Troublette *(s. brewery p.124)*

Hiding behind this cute little name is a craft White Beer, brewed by Caracole in Falmignoul, near Dinant. It apparently takes its name from the characteristics of its non-filtered, wheat based beer. Troublette is also released in an "écolo" ("ecological") version, logically called *Troublette Bio*.

Troublette

Top fermentation – White Beer

🍺 blond – yellow, cloudy

📷 Brasserie Caracole, Falmignoul (Namur)

% 5

This White Beer actually has a blond body, only slightly cloudy, an abundant head that holds well and presents a significant release

of gasses. In the nose, it develops scents of lemon and orange blossom. In the mouth it is a little piquant and reveals notes of orange blossom, lemon and a light, balanced bitterness. It has a certain pungent quality in its finish.

Val-Dieu (s. brewery p.121)

Relatively discrete at a time when Abbey beers are making a come back in the media, the beers of Val-Dieu were launched by a small family brewery from the Herve country in 1993. The Piron brewery, founded in 1907 and otherwise considered one of the most technically proficient in the Walloon region, had closed its doors in the early 1970s. But, under pressure from his children, Joseph Piron consented to return to service and produced an inspired and improved version of the beer of the Val-Dieu monks. Facilities had to be re-built, since the law disallowed a non-operating brewery to maintain its equipment. The adventure was short lived though, since the Piron brewery declared bankruptcy and was put into liquidation in 1997. However, the beer didn't suffer, since its production continued... on the same site as the abbey but under the direction of a new company.

Thanks to this operation, the beer of the Val-Dieu abbey is the only "Beer of a Recognized Abbey" that is produced in a functioning abbey. As for the Cistercian community Notre Dame de Val-Dieu, tucked in tranquillity deep in the valley of the Berwinne, it was founded in 1216 at the request of the Duke of Limbourg. It has more or less resisted the ravages of time and revolutions. A dairy in the vicinity also produces a cheese that has absolutely nothing in common with its analogous counterparts.

Since 7 April 2000, a museum of art and history has held its doors open thanks to the care of those who organized such benefits as "J'avais 20 ans en 45" ("I was 20 years old in 45") or those for Hergé and Simenon in the last few years. Judging by the success of these expositions, the 150.000 annual visitors mark will not be hard for them to reach. In other news, negotiations are underway to propose a tasting room totally autonomous from the ecclesiastical activities.

Despite its limited production, Val-Dieu is present in the principle European countries.

Val-Dieu Blonde

Top fermentation – Abbey

blond

Brasserie de l'Abbaye de Val-Dieu, Aubel (Liège)

% 6,5

Tasting notes

A yellow beer, slightly cloudy and with a persistent head, Val Dieu Blond develops complex aromas of cream, nuts, hops, coriander and cloves. It presents a certain acidity, deepened by a light touch of lemon.

Val-Dieu Brune

Top fermentation – Abbey

brown

Brasserie de l'Abbaye de Val-Dieu, Aubel (Liège)

% 8

Tasting notes

Val Dieu Brune releases aromas of pure chocolate, coffee, nougat, passion fruit and grape.

Pub secret

During the 80s, the monks of the Val-Dieu abbey made contact with the Piron brewery, nearby the abbey, because they wanted a beer to be produced under their symbol. Funny, since we know that Philippe Piron, father of the "creator" of Val-Dieu beer, had already in 1963, proposed the same association. The representatives of the abbey had then refused...

Vieux-Temps *(s. brewery p.130)*

An amber beer, previously brewed at the Saint-Guibert brewery in Mont-Saint-Guibert – like the Leffe – it has since then passed into the fold of Interbrew. Its name and character are intended to evoke the beers of the early XXth century. It also seems that the number one Belgian brewer hasn't made a priority of developing Vieux-Temps.

Vieux-Temps

Top fermentation – Ale

amber

Brouwerij Interbrew, Leuven (Flemish Brabant)

% 5

Tasting notes

Of an amber colour, with red highlights, Vieux-Temps offers a nice compact head that is short lived. It presents a nose of barley and hops. Soft in the mouth, it distinguishes itself with an aroma of caramel and liquorice. It finishes with a bitterness that is light and short.

Villers (s. brewery p.130)

The Villers-la-Ville abbey, in Brabant Wallon, is one of the most prestigious sites of gothic ruins in Belgium. Like most of the abbeys in Belgium, it can justify its production of beer for the consumption of the monks that live there. The Cistercian monastery was founded in 1146 and was, up until its destruction in 1793, one of the places of highest Christian spirituality in our region. It is still a pleasant place to go to and wander among, and admire, architectural vestiges from the XIIIth to the XVIIIth century.

Maybe this is what made the Huyghe brewery decide to take up the brewing of Villers, produced up until 1999 by a brewery in Puurs, in the province of Anvers. In any case, it is an operation that allows the last of 300 breweries having existed in Gand, to battle on.

It all started in 1902 when Léon Huyghe moved himself to Melle to take a job in a local brewery. He worked there four years before... he bought the business. It was called, at that time, Brewery-Malt House "den Appel" and kept that name until 1938, when it became S.A. Léon Huyghe. The War and its rationing created the curious opportunity to brew a beer using a French variety of hops, Kenia Gold, that came about in 1945. And, in 1948, Albert Huyghe, son of Léon, added the production of soft drinks. In 1980, Jean De Laet, son-in-law of Albert, arrived at the helm of the enterprise and breathed in a considerable amount of new life. He developed a series of new beers, aided by his son, and followed up by transforming the family business into a modern enterprise, specialising in top fermentations and resolutely turned towards the export market.

Villers Triple

Top fermentation – Abbey

🍺 blond

🏭 Brouwerij Huyghe, Melle (East Flanders)

% 8,5

Tasting notes

This beer is a light amber, and develops a persistent head. It presents a nose of Madeira and fruit to which is added notes of honey and caramel. Round and full in the mouth, it diffuses touches of pronounced malt and hops. Soft, it delivers aromas of honey, pepper, and offers a nice prolonged bitterness. It is a fairly complex beer that also reveals notes of apple and apricot. It is slightly piquant in the mouth, and finishes bitter.

Pub secret

On a visit to the abbey at Villers-la-Ville, you might be able to attend one of the theatrical performances held there each summer. The enchanting environment lends itself beautifully to this sort of thing. Another curiosity, if one can call it that, of this set of ruins, comes from the Charleroi-Ottignies rail line that passes right through the grounds : you can see there a building literally cut in two, a symptom of a time when we thought much less of these types of details...

Villers (Vieille)

Top fermentation – Abbey

🍺 brown

📷 Brouwerij Huyghe, Melle (East Flanders)

% 7

Tasting notes

This is a brown, presenting an abundant head that holds well, with a significant release of gasses. Sweetness, malt and caramel characterise its nose. In the mouth, it is a little piquant, and calls back each time malt, a certain roasting, mocha, liquorice and a light, prolonged bitterness.

Westmalle *(s. brewery p.121)*

The creation of the Westmalle abbey is, one might say, a direct consequence of the French Revolution since the Cistercians that occupy it come originally from Normandy. An exodus, of sorts, though we know that Robespierre and his friends didn't fool around with these types of matters. Within the boundaries of the province of Anvers, a cannon-ball's flight from the border of Holland, the Westmalle abbey has rested since 1794, that is just after the heretical period of the *sans-culottes*.

It is the oldest active Trappist brewery since its first vat was obtained in 1836. They brew two models of beer, a double (the only Trappist also available in casks) and a triple, the monks having, for themselves, their own beer (light) for everyday drinking, sometimes available for tasting at the brewery. Works are underway to replace the bottling and production areas with a new ultra modern facility. It should be finished by the end of this year.

Westmalle Dubbel

Top fermentation – Trappist

🍺 dark brown

📷 Abdij der Trappisten, Westmalle (Anvers)

% 6,5

Tasting notes

A dark brown beer with an average effervescence and a head that holds well, creamy and abundant, the Westmalle Double presents a floral and winy nose. Piquant in the mouth, one distinguishes flavours of roasting, mocha, liquorice, notes of pear, banana and toasted bread.

Westmalle Tripel

Top fermentation – Trappist

🍺 amber

📷 Abdij der Trappisten, Westmalle (Anvers)

% 9

Tasting notes

Presenting a beautiful blond colour a little cloudy and with a compact, short lived head, the Westmalle Triple also offers a fruity and herby nose, accompanied by notes of fresh hops. Round in the mouth, it develops a powerful bitterness followed by flavours of lemon and caramel, rock candy, sage and orange.

🍽 asparagus, artichoke, tart "al Djote", streaky bacon

Pub secret

A monk from the Westmalle abbey confided one day, without a smile, to the celebrated *beer chaser* M. Jackson, that the only beer that could properly accompany asparagus was the Westmalle Triple...

Westvleteren (s. brewery p.121)

It is the most rare (before the arrival of Achel) and the most mysterious of the Trappists, without a doubt. The monks, wanting to respect the Cistercian rules to the letter, have never given the brewery the headway to produce the beer in large quantity. Therefore, one doesn't find the beer except at the doors of the abbey and one or two cafés in the immediate area. And if, by chance, someone offers you one elsewhere, it is most likely a pretender, the exception, as always, confirming the rule.

A point of supplemental originality, the Westvleteren bottles come without a label (differentiated only by their stoppers) and in antique wooden crates. The monks offer to the public two beers with similar characteristics, though they also produce a third, for their own everyday consumption.

Westvleteren Abt 12

Top fermentation – Trappist

🍺 dark brown

📷 Abdij St Sixtus, West-Vleteren (West Flanders)

% 12

Tasting notes

A strong brown body, and abundant head that holds well and a significant release of gasses defines the visual aspect. To the nose, it is powerful, offering notes of pear and banana and a complex fruitiness. In the mouth, it is acidic, strong, calling up mocha and liquorice and presenting a strong, prolonged bitterness, with traces of roasting and a certain pungency in the finish.

Pub secret

Present in the area since 1831, the monks had the opportunity to buy a used brewery in 1838. It cost them 919 francs. No doubt they wanted to see if their "sauce" would take before they went too far. In this case, the adage about the best soups being made in the oldest pots seems to ring true.

Westvleteren Extra 8

Top fermentation – Trappist

🍺 dark brown

📷 Abdij St Sixtus, West-Vleteren (West Flanders)

% 8,1

Tasting notes

The Westvleteren 8 is fairly fruity. It reveals notes of cognac and almond in a finish that is relatively dry. Served between 15 and 18. It develops an abundant head that holds well and an average effervescence. It leaves a prolonged bitterness.

🧀 soft cheese

Westvleteren Spéciale 6

Top fermentation – Trappist

Production has been halted since the beginning of 1999

Witkap Pater (s. brewery p.134)

The Slaghmuylder brewery was born in 1860, thanks to Emmanuel Slaghmuylder, until then a grains broker. His son took over the reins of the family business as the XXth century dawned and married Marie Van Roy, daughter of the Wieze brewers. He acquired a larger site, on which his three sons built a new brewery in 1925. The following year, they launched a beer of bottom fermentation, then all the rage. But, they abandoned this technique with the Second World War in order to save money. They took advantage of the World Exposition (1958) to again brew a Pilsner and other derivatives.

The three sons took over in the middle of the sixties, each controlling a well defined sector of the business. Philippe headed up administrative management, Michel concentrated on production and acquisitions, and Everard carried out technical services and sales. Under their direction, the brewery gave birth to Witkap Pater (White-cloaked Father) in 1979. Initially brewed for the "Les Trois Tilleuls" brewery in Brasschaat (Anvers), it entered the Slaghmuylder fold in 1981. It is available in three versions : a Double, a "Stimulo", blond and light, bubbly like champagne, and a Triple, by popular demand the most suc-

cessful. They also market a series of other beers, running from a Pilsner to table beer, in addition to, like some of their competitors, a range of soft drinks and waters. And, they are the lucky owners of a steam engine, still in working order.

Witkap Pater Tripel

Top fermentation – Abbey

🍺 blond

📛 Brouwerij Slaghmuylder, Ninove (East Flanders)

% 7,5

Tasting notes

The *Witkap* Triple presents, under a weak head that holds poorly, a slightly cloudy, blond body. The release of gasses is average while the nose wraps itself in barley and hops. It is a little tart in the mouth, hops is present and it develops a nice

Brasserie SLAGHMUYLDER
9400 Ninove
Tél. : 054/33 18 31 – Fax : 33.84.45

bitterness that is balanced and prolonged. One tastes also some touches of bay laurel.

Pub secret

Like many other beers in its category, the Witkap Pater is re-fermented in the bottle, which means it undergoes a third fermentation. The yeasts will eventually fall to the bottom of the bottle or keg, leaving the beer clear. But, if the *Witkap* is over chilled, it will become cloudy again. The cause ; egg white, used to clarify it, which coagulates.

Wittekerke *(s. brewery p.122)*

Top fermentation - Other

🍺 pale, cloudy

🏭 Brouwerij Bavik, bavikhove (West Flanders)

% 5

Tasting notes

A true Wit (white) beer must be made of at least 25 % wheat malt in combination with barley malt. Wittekerke is the last Belgian Wit that also uses a small amount of oats. Belgian Wit beers are naturally cloudy since they are unfiltered. Wittekerke is the fruitiest (slight hints of lemon) of the Belgian Wits, very refreshing and pleasant to drink, and was voted 2 years in a row the best Belgian Wit by Belgian consumers (Test Aankoop). It charms you with its own character, smooth taste and unique delicious aroma. A very pleasant drink, light in alcohol with a crisp and refreshing flavor, you'll find a perfect white head.

Wittekerke is a fictitious name for a typical Flemish town, like we find many villages in Flanders with a name ending on KERKE (church). Witte means white in English, thus the translation of the name is White Church. Since the mid 1990's, a very popular soap on Belgian TV has adopted the same name. The actors drink Wittekerke on screen, which helps to promote the Wittekerke beer.

Drink Wittekerke at parties and receptions, or combine it with a spicy carpaccio, with scallops, or with a fresh salad.

Zulte *(s. brewery p.121)*

These browns, characteristic of Flanders, used to be brewed in Zulte, a large village near Waregen (East Flanders) from which it took its name. Today, it has entered into the control of the Alken-Maes group, thereby becoming a cousin to Grimbergen. Its entry "among the greats" has at least allowed Zulte to escape its confines and to exercise its prerogatives far from its home territory. This notoriety is amply merited, because in addition to its thirst quenching properties, Zulte is a veritable alternative to certain other, more famous products.

Zulte

Top fermentation – Flemish Brown

🍺 red - brown

🏭 Brouwerij Alken-Maes, Waarloos (Anvers)

% 4,7

Tasting notes

A dark brown beer, with a short lived head, it presents an average release of gasses while its nose is fruity and sweet. In the mouth, it is piquant and acidic with a light bitterness.

BREWERIES

It has been said and repeated, but it's always nice to hear: Belgium is THE home of beers above all else, in number, variety and wide range of tastes. Some are distributed widely, even nationally and internationally, while others are distributed only locally. However, take note of the fact that the majority are still locally produced, and destined for the local population.

The breweries presented below are a representative selection of the Belgian brewing landscape, but this list is in no way exhaustive. The beers in **bold text** are those presented in detail. The parenthetical remarks are the category to which the beer belongs.

ABBAYE DES ROCS

Chaussée Brunehault, 3
7387 Montignies-sur-Roc
Tel.: 065/75 59 99
Fax: 065/75 59 98
e-mail:
abbaye-des-rocs@skynet.be
http://www.abbaye-des-rocs.com
Tour by reservation, price: 60 BEF

Abbaye des Rocs (Abbey)

La Montagnarde (Abbey)

Abbaye des Rocs Spéciale Noël (Abbey)

Blanche des Honnelles (White)

ABBAYE DE VAL-DIEU

Val Dieu, 225
4880 Aubel
Tel.: 087/68 75 87
Fax: 087/68 79 58
Tour consists of a video presentation and 25 minute tasting, price: 100 BEF

Val Dieu Blonde (Abbey)
Val Dieu Brune (Abbey)

ABBAYE NOTRE DAME ST. RÉMY

Rue de l'Abbaye, 8
5580 Rochefort
Tel.: 084/22 01 40
Rochefort 6 (Trappist)
Rochefort 8 (Trappist)
Rochefort 10 (Trappist)

ABDIJ DER TRAPPISTEN

Antwerpsesteenweg, 496
2390 Westmalle
Tel.: 03/312 92 22
Fax: 03/312 92 27
e-mail:
info@trappistwestmalle.be
Westmalle Dubbel (Trappist)
Westmalle Tripel (Trappist)

ABDIJ ST. SIXTUS

Donkerstraat, 12
8640 Westvleteren
Tel.: 057/40 03 76

Fax: 057/40 14 20
Westvleteren 6 (Trappist)
Westvleteren 8 (Trappist)
Westvleteren 10 (Trappist)

ACHOUFFE

Achouffe, 32
6666 Achouffe
Tel.: 061/28 81 47
Fax: 061/28 82 64
http://www.achouffe.be
Tours by reservation for group of 10 to 40, price: 150 BEF, tasting included

Achouffe (Special)
Mc Chouffe (Special)
Chouffe Bock 6666 (Special)
N'Ice Chouffe (Special Noël)

ALKEN-MAES

Waarloosveld, 10
2550 Waarloos-Kontich
Tel.: 015/30 90 11
Fax: 015/31 41 91
http://www.maes.be
Tours free year-round, Tuesday and Thursday from 1400h to 1700h

Maes Pils (Pilsner)
Zulte (Flemish Brown)
Cristal (Pilsner)
Kronenbourg (Pilsner)
Maes Nature (table beer)
Tourtel (non-alcoholic beer)

Other sites

ALKEN-MAES
Stationsstraat, 2
3570 Alken
Tel.: 011/59 03 00
Fax: 011/59 03 01
Beers in casks or kegs
Tours free all year from Tuesday through Thursday, 1400h to 1700h

DE KEERSMAKER
Lierput, 1
1730 Kobegem
Tel.: 02/452 63 24
Fax: 02/452 43 10
Mort Subite Gueuze
(spontaneous fermentation)
Mort Subite Kriek *(Cherry)*
(spontaneous fermentation)
Mort Subite Framboise
(Raspberry)
(spontaneous fermentation)
Mort Subite, gueuze sur lie
(spontaneous fermentation)
Mort Subite Pêche – *(Peach)*
(spontaneous fermentation)
Mort Subite Cassis – *(Black-currant)*
(spontaneous fermentation)

UNION
Rue Derbècque, 7
6040 Jumet
Tel.: 071/34 02 22
Fax: 071/34 02 34
Ciney Blonde (Special)
Ciney Brune (Special)
Ciney Spéciale (Special)
Cuvée de l'Ermitage (Abbey)
Grimbergen Dubbel (Abbey)
Grimbergen Tripel (Abbey)
Grimbergen Optimo Bruno (Abbey)
Grimbergen Blonde (Abbey)
Judas (Special)

BAVIK

Rijksweg, 33
8531 Bavikhove (Harelbeke)
Tel.: 056/71 90 91
Fax: 056/71 15 12
e-mail:
http://www.bavik.be
Tours by reservation

Bavik Pils (Pilsner)
Petrus Old Brown (Flemish Brown)
Petrus Triple (Special)
Petrus Speciale (Special)

Wittekerke (White)

BOCKOR NV

Kwabrugstraat, 5
8510 Bellegem (Kortrijk)
Tel.: 056/23 51 71
Fax: 056/22 76 83
e-mail:
http://www.bockor.be
Jacobins Lambic

BOON FRANK

Fonteinstraat, 65
1502 Lembeek
Tel.: 02/356 66 44
Fax: 02/356 33 99
Guided tours in July and August at 1500h on Wednesday, price: 100 BEF including tasting. The meeting point is next to the Lembeek church at the " De Kring " café. Reservation required and available at 02/356 42 59 or 02/356 54 11

Boon Geuze (spontaneous fermentation)
Boon Kriek (spontaneous fermentation)
Boon Framboise (spontaneous fermentation)

BOSTEELS

Kerkstraat, 96
9255 Buggenhout
Tel.: 052/33 22 82
Fax: 052/33 59 56
Tours available with arrangement Monday through Friday, price: 150 BEF including tasting.

Kwak (Special)
Triple Karmeliet (Special)
'T Zelfde —*La Même Chose*— (Special)

CANTILLON

rue Gheude, 56
1070 Bruxelles
Tel.: 02/521 49 28
Fax: 02/520 28 91
Cantillon Gueuze (spontaneous fermentation)
Cantillon Kriek (spontaneous fermentation)
Rosé de Gambrinus (spontaneous fermentation)
Cantillon Faro (spontaneous fermentation)
Iris (spontaneous fermentation)

CARACOLE

Côte Marie-Thérèse, 86
5500 Falmignoul
Tel.: 082/74 40 80
Fax: 082/74 52 38
Nostradamus 9,5° (Special) ex cuvée de l'an neuf
Caracole Ambrée (Special)
Saxo (Special)
Troublette (White)
Tours every day in July and August in the afternoon, price: 150 BEF. The rest of the year, with arrangement for groups. Tours include tasting of three beers.

CHIMAY

Route Charlemagne, 8
6464 Baileux
Tel.: 060/21 03 11
Fax: 060/21 34 22
e-mail: info@chimay.be
http://www.chimay.be
Tours of the bottling site Tuesday through Friday from 0900h to 1300h, with reservation for groups of 15 at a minimum. Tours for individuals Tuesday through Friday at 1000h from the 15th of June through the 15th of September, including a video, tour of the site and tasting.

Chimay Bleue *(Blue)* (Trappist)
Chimay Rouge *(Red)* (Trappist)
Chimay Triple (Trappist)
Chimay Première (Trappist)
Chimay Grande Réserve (Trappist)
Chimay Cinq Cents *(Five Hundred)* (Trappist)

CLARYSSE

Krekelput, 18
9700 Oudenaarde
Tel.: 055/31 17 21
Fax : 055/31 94 76
Felix (old brown)
St. Hermes (Abbey)

Brasserie
La Caracole

86, Côte Marie-Thérèse • 5500 Falmignoul (Dinant) • Belgique
Tél. : +32(0)82 / 74 40 80 • Fax : +32(0)82 / 74 52 38

Visit the bottling plant of the Trappist Beers of Chimay

Guided tours for individuals from Tuesday till Friday, from 15/06 to 15/09.

Guided tours for groups of at least 15 persons all over the year (by appointment) from Tuesday till Friday, between 9:00 a.m. and 1:30 p.m.

This visit will start with the showing of a film describing the complete brewing and cheese making processes.

After the film, you will tour through the bottling plant with a digital headphone system and then through the cheese making plant.

And not to leave thirsty, you will be able to taste some Chimay products offered by the company Bières de Chimay.

For further information, please contact Helena Rolies.
Bières de Chimay
Route Charlemagne, 8 - 6464 Baileux (Chimay)
Phone.: 060/21.03.11 - Fax: 060/21.34.22

CNUDDE

Fabriekstraat, 8
9700   Eine
Tel.: 055/31 18 34
Cnudde Kriek

CROMBE

Hospitaalstraat, 10
9620   Zottegem
Tel.: 091/36 00 24
Oud Zottegems

DE BIE

Stoppelweg, 26
8978   Watou
Tel.: 057/38 86 66
Hellekapelle
Zatte Bie

DE BLOCK

Nieuwbaan, 92
1785   Merchtem
Tel.: 052/37 21 59
Fax: 052/37 53 88
Tours available with reservation, including entry to the small brewery museum, price 20 BEF including tasting.

Satan Red (Special)
Satan Gold (Special)
Kastaar (Special)
Triple Dendermonde (Special)

DE BRUNEHAUT

Rue des Panneries, 17-19
7623   Rongy (Brunehaut)
Tel.: 069/34 64 11
Fax: 069/34 64 12
Brunehaut (blond & amber)
Mont St. Aubert
Ne Kopstoot

DE DOLLE BROUWERS

Roeselarestraat, 128
8600   Diksmuide
Tel.: 051/50 27 81
Fax: 051/51 03 37

Arabier
Oerbier
Stille Nacht

DE GOUDEN BOOM (Gr. Alken-Maes)

Langestraat, 45
8000   Brugge
Tel.: 050/33 06 99
Fax: 050/33 46 44
e-mail: info@degoudenboom.com
http://www.degoudenboom.com
Brugs Tarwebier (White)
Brugse Tripel (Special)
Steenbrugge Dubbel (Abbey)
Steenbrugge Tripel (Abbey)

DE KONINCK

Mechelsesteenweg, 291
2018   Antwerpen
Tel.: 03/218 40 48
Fax: 03/230 85 19
e-mail: info@dekoninck.com
http://www.dekoninck.com
Tours available (except July and August), price: 2500 BEF for 25 people

De Koninck (Ale)
Cuvée De Koninck (Ale)
Antoon (Ale)
De Koninck Christmas (Special Noël)

DE LANDTSHEER NV

Mandekensstraat, 179
9255   Buggenhout
Tel.: 052/33 39 11
Fax: 052/34 25 28
e-mail: delandtsheer@malheur.be
http://www.malheur.be
Malheur

DE RYCK

Kerkstraat, 28
9550   Herzele
Tel.: 053/62 23 02
Fax: 053/63 15 41
De Ryck (Special)

DE SMEDT

Ringlaan, 18
1745 Opwijk
Tel.: 052/35 99 11
Fax: 052/35 83 57
Affligem Blond (Abbey)
Affligem Dubbel (Abbey)
Affligem Tripel (Abbey)
Postel Dubbel (Abbey)
Postel Tripel (Abbey)
Affligem Christmas (Abbey)
Affligem Patersvat (Abbey)
Bières Delhaize
Celis White (White)
Op-Ale (Ale)
Postel Kerstbier (Special Noël)

DE TROCH

Langestraat, 20
1741 Ternat
Tel.: 02/582 10 27
Fax: 02/582 72 41
e-mail: detroch@unicall.be
Chapeau banana *(banana)* (spontaneous fermentation)
Chapeau exotic (spontaneous fermentation)
Chapeau fraise *(strawberry)* (spontaneous fermentation)
Chapeau abricot *(apricot)* (spontaneous fermentation)
Chapeau faro (spontaneous fermentation)
Chapeau framboise *(raspberry)* (spontaneous fermentation)
Chapeau gueuze (spontaneous fermentation)
Chapeau kriek *(cherry)* (spontaneous fermentation)
Chapeau lemon (spontaneous fermentation)
Chapeau mirabelle (spontaneous fermentation)
Chapeau pêche *(peach)* (spontaneous fermentation)
Cuvée Chapeau (spontaneous fermentation)

DU BOCQ

Rue de la Brasserie, 4
5530 Purnode
Tel.: 082/61 07 90
Fax: 082/61 17 80
e-mail: brasserie@bocq.be
http://www.bocq.be
Tours lasting 50 minutes for groups of 20 people minimum, with reservation, available all year; individual tours daily in July and August from 1400h to 1600h (from the 1st of April to the 30th of June and from the 1st to the 30th of September, tours at 1500h on the weekends, holidays and school breaks); price: 150 BEF including a tasting (100 BEF per person for groups).

The brewery also organizes day long programs: détente et plaisir au programme.
Blanche de Namur (White)
Corsendonk Agnus (Abby)
La Gauloise Ambrée (Special)
La Gauloise Blonde (Special)
La Gauloise Brune (Special)
St Feuillien Blonde (Abbey)
x^2 (Abbey)
Blanche de Noël (Special Noël)
Triple Moine or Saint-Benoit Triple or Deugniet (Abbey)
Régal Christmas (Special Noël)
Saison Régal (seasonal)

DUBUISSON

Chaussée de Mons, 28
7904 Pipaix
Tel.: 069/67 22 22
Fax: 069/66 17 27
e-mail: info@br-dubuisson.com
http://www.br-dubuisson.com
Tours available, price 50 BEF including video and tasting. Group tours available through the Tournai office of tourism (069/22 20 45)

Bush Ambrée (Special)

Bush 7 (Special)
Bush Blonde (Special)
Bush de Noël (Special Noël)

DUPONT

Rue Basse, 5
7904 Tourpes
Tel.: 069/67 10 66
Fax: 069/66 17 27
Tours with reservation for groups of 35 to 60 people including tour of site, video on beer production and tasting of two glasses of Moinette accompanied by cheese; price: 100 BEF per person.

Moinette Blonde (Special)
Moinette Brune (Special)
Moinette biologique (Special)
Dupont biologique (Special)
Dupont Vieille provision (Special)

DUVEL MOORTGAT

Breendonkdorp, 58
2870 Breendonk
Tel.: 03/860 94 00
Fax: 03/886 46 22
e-mail: info@duvel.be
http://www.duvel.be
Free tours Tuesday, Wednesday and Thursday at 0930h and at 1400h, comprised of a video, facilities tour and tasting.

Duvel Rouge (Special)
Maredsous 6 Blonde (Abbey)
Maredsous 6 Brune (Abbey)
Maredsous 8 (Abbey)
Maredsous 10 (Abbey)
Bel Pils (Pilsner)
Duvel Verte (Special)
Godefroy (Special)
Passendale(Special)

DES FAGNES

Route de Nismes, 26
5660 Mariembourg
Tel.: 060/31 39 19

Fax: 060/31 19 40
e-mail:
mail@brasseriedesfagnes.be
http://www.brasseriedesfagnes.be
Free tours every day from April through October, 1000h to 2100h, from November to March, 1500h to 2100h during the week (1000h to 2100h weekends and holidays); closed Monday. Group tours with reservation, price: 180 BEF including complete guided tour (trilingual), tasting and a souvenir glass.

In the same building as the modern brewery, a brewery dating from 1858 has been reconstructed. The materials came from the Degauquier de Chimay brewery which ceased production in 1977. Here you'll find ancient vats and a lorry used for deliveries. Interactive terminals guide the visitor through the new as well as the old areas. This site hosted 130.000 visitors in 1999.

On site, one may also discover and taste other artisanal products such as cheese made by local artisans, sausages, de l'escavèche,...

Super des Fagnes (Special)
Beers of the week

ELLEZELLOISE

Guinaumont, 75
7890 Ellezelles
Tel.: 068/54 31 60
Fax: 068/54 37 16
Quintine (Special)
Quintine de Noël (Special Noël)

FANTOME

Rue Preal, 8
6997 Soy
Tel.: 086/47 70 44
Fantôme

FRIART (Brasserie du Roeulx)

Rue d'Houdeng, 20
7070 Le Roeulx
Tel.: 064/66 21 51
Fax: 064/67 67 30
e-mail:
brasserie.friart@skynet.be
http://www.stfeuillien.com
Tours by appointment for groups of 15 to 40, Tuesday through Sunday, price: 150 BEF including two tastings.

Grisette Ambrée (Special)
St-Feuillien Blonde (Abbey)
St-Feuillien Brune (Abbey)
Grisette Blanche (Special)
Grisette Blonde (Special)
St Feuillien cuvée de Noël (Special Noël)
St Feuillien Triple (Abbey)

GIRARDIN

Lindenbergstraat, 10-12
1700 Sint-Ulriks-Kapelle
Tel.: 02/452 64 19
Fax: 02/453 94 19
Girardin Lambic

GOUDEN CAROLUS

Guido Gezellelaan, 49
2800 Mechelen
Tel.: 015/20 38 80
Fax: 015/21 21 07
Gouden Carolus

HAACHT

Provinciesteenweg, 28
3190 Boortmeerbeek
Tel.: 016/60 15 01
Fax: 016/60 83 84
e-mail: info@primus.be
http://www.primus.be
Tours by written request only (letter, fax or e-mail), for groups of at least 20, Monday through Thursday (afternoon). It is free and includes two tastings in the establishment across the street from the brewery. There they serve a " Primus met gist ". an unfiltered pilsner with yeast sediment, as well as elaborate regional dishes based on beer. The Haacht brewery also has a museum that shows the diverse elements of the brewery as of 1924.

Visitors are welcomed into an ultra modern brewing room, controlled entirely by computer. Its maximum capacity is 7200hl per day. A show of lights and sounds enlivens the atmosphere.

Blanche de Haacht (White)
Charles Quint (Special)
Primus Haacht (Pilsner)
Tongerlo Dubbel (Abbey)
Tongerlo Dubbel Blond (Abbey)

www.primus.be

Primus
Bottom fermentation beer of 5,2 % Vol. Alc. with a particular refreshing flavour.

Tongerlo blond 6°, brown 6° and tripel 8°
Authentic top fermentation abbey beers with refermentation in the bottle.

Charles Quint
Very special top fermentation beer of 9 % Vol. Alc. Mild and fruity.

ANNO 1898
BROUWERIJ
HAACHT
BRASSERIE

Provinciesteenweg 28 B-3190
tel:+32 (0)16/601.501 fax:+32 (0)16/60.83.84
e-mail: info@primus.be

Tongerlo Tripel (Abbey)

Adler (Pilsner)

Tongerlo Christmas (Special Noël)

HET ANKER

Guido Gezellestraat, 49
2800 Mechelen
Tel.: 015/20 38 80
Fax: 015/21 21 07
Tours of 10 persons minimum, 125 BEF including tasting. The tour is an interactive conception, between installations of the old and the new, brewing of yesterday and today.

Gouden Carolus or *Carolus d'Or* (Special)

Cuvée van de Keizer (Special)

Brune de Malines (Special)

Triple Toison d'Or (Special)

Den Blusser (Pilsner)

HUYGHE – VAN MELLE

Brusselsesteenweg, 282
9090 Melle
Tel.: 09/252 15 01
Fax: 09/252 29 31
e-mail: delirium@delirium.be
http://www.delirium.be
Tours by appointment for groups of 12 or more, price: 125 BEF including tasting. A completely new tasting room was recently inaugurated. One may see there fresco murals, ancient brewing tools and a family collection of pitchers and beer steins from all over.

Delirium Nocturnum (Special)

Delirium Tremens (Special)

VieilleVillers (Abbey)

Villers Triple (Abbey)

gamme Floris (Special)

St Idesbald Blonde (Special)

St Idesbald Brune (Special)

INTERBREW

Grand'Place, 1
1000 Bruxelles
Tel.: 02/514 10 60
Fax: 02/514 54 92
http://www.bestbelgianbeers.com

Other sites

INTERBREW BELGIUM
Rue des Anciennes Houblonnières, 2
4020 Jupille-sur-Meuse
Tel.: 04/345 82 11
Fax: 04/345 86 08
Tours free Monday through Friday at)930h, 1330h and 1500h including a video, tour of the facility and tasting. For reservations 04/345 87 55

Jupiler (Pilsner)

Leffe (Abbey)

Bières Derby (Pilsner)

INTERBREW BELGIUM
Vaartstraat, 94
3000 Leuven
Tel.: 016/24 71 11
Fax: 016/24 74 07
Free tours available Monday through Friday at 0930h, 1330h and 1500h

Jupiler **N.A.** (Non-alcoholic beer)

Leffe Blonde (Abbey)

Leffe Brune (Abbey)

Leffe Radieuse (Abbey)

Leffe Triple (Abbey)

Stella Artois (Pilsner)

Stella **N.A.** (Non-alcoholic beer)

Vieux-Temps (Ale)

Bières Piedboeuf (table beer)

Loburg (Pilsner deluxe)

Safir (Pilsner)

Supra Pils (Pilsner)

Stella light (Pilsner)

Tuborg (Pilsner deluxe)

Wiel's (Pilsner)

DE KLUIS
Stoopkensstraat, 46
3320 Hoegaarden
Tel.: 016/76 98 11
Fax: 016/76 76 91
Free tours including two tastings, Monday through Saturday at 1030h, 1330h, 1500h and 1630h.

Blanche   de   Hoegaarden (White)
Hoegaarden Spéciale (White)
Hoegaarden Grand Cru (Special)
Fruit Défendu (Special)
Julius (Special)
Hoegaardse Das (Ale)

BELLE-VUE
Bergensesteenweg, 144
1600 Sint-Pieters-Leeuw
Tel.: 02/371 43 00
Fax: 02/371 43 66
Quai du Hainaut, 33
1080 Molenbeek
Tel.: 02/410 19 35
Tel.: 02/410 78 58
Free guided tours including a gueuze and choice of another beer, Monday through Friday at 0930h, 1100h, 1330h, 1500h. No tours Tuesday mornings or Saturday at 1500h.

Gueuze Belle-Vue (spontaneous fermentation)
Kriek Belle-Vue (spontaneous fermentation)
Framboise Belle-Vue (spontaneous fermentation)
De Neve Gueuze (spontaneous fermentation)
De Neve Kriek (spontaneous fermentation)
De Neve Framboise (spontaneous fermentation)
Jack-Op (spontaneous fermentation)
Kriek Primeur (spontaneous fermentation)

LA BINCHOISE
Rue Faubourg St Paul, 38
7130 Binche
Tel.: 064/33 61 86
Fax: 064/33 61 86
e-mail:
brasserie.la.binchoise@skynet.be
Guided tours of the facility for groups of 15 minimum, public brewing every first Saturday of the month beginning at 0800h. Tasting room, in which one can find regional dishes supplied from the kitchen, also open to weekend walk-ins from 1500h. An "Open House" weekend is hosted as well, where one may discover the "Rose des Remparts" (Rose of the Ramparts).

Associated with the neighbouring Friart brewery, the Binchoise was included by the 'S.I. Régional du Centre' in the "Circuit of Beer and Folklore". For 520 BEF per person (groups of 15 to 30 people), this guided tour includes tours of the two brewing facilities, entrance to the Museum of Carnival and Masquerade and beer tastings. Information available from 064/26 15 00.

Binchoise Blonde (Special)
Bière des Ours (Special)
Bière de Pâques (Springtime (Easter) Special)
Binchoise Brune (Special)
Binchoise Spéciale Noël (Special Noël)
Rose des Remparts (Special)

LEFÈBVRE
Rue du Croly, 54
1430 Quenast
Tel.: 067/67 07 66
Fax: 067/67 02 38
e-mail: sealineakil@hotmail.be
Barbar (Special)

Abbaye de Bonne Espérance (Abbey)
Bières de l'Abbaye de Floreffe (Abbey)
Blanche de Bruxelles (White)
Newton (White infused with apple)
Saison 1900 (seasonal)

LINDEMANS

Lenniksebaan, 1479
1602 Vlezenbeek
Tel.: 02/569 03 90
Fax: 02/569 05 10
http://www.lindemans.be
Lindemans Gueuze (spontaneous fermentation)
Lindemans Kriek *(cherry)* (spontaneous fermentation)
Lindemans Framboise *(raspberry)* (spontaneous fermentation)
Lindemans cassis *(blackcurrant)* (spontaneous fermentation)
Lindemans faro (spontaneous fermentation)
Pécheresse (spontaneous fermentation)
Tea Beer (spontaneous fermentation)

LOUWAEGE

Markt, 14
8610 Kortemarkt
Tel.: 051/56 60 67
Fax: 051/57 05 95
e-mail: info@hapkin.be
Hapkin (Special)
Akila Pilsener (Pilsner)
Flandrien (Special)
Louwaege's Pils (Pilsner)

MARTENS

Reppelerweg, 1
3950 Bocholt
Tel.: 089/47 29 80
Fax: 089/47 27 00
Tours of the brewery free, including a tasting.

Martens Pils (Pilsner)
Sezeons (seasonal)

ORVAL

Abbaye Notre-Dame d'Orval
6823 Villers-Devant-Orval
Tel.: 061/31 12 61
Fax: 061/31 29 27
e-mail:
dir.commercial.brasserie@orval.be
http://www.orval.be
The brewery is open, during the week and by appointment, only to professionals of the industry.
Orval (Trappist)
Petite Bière or *Orval Verte* (Trappist)

PALM

Steenhuffeldorp, 3
1840 Steenhuffel
Tel.: 052/30 94 81
Fax: 052/30 41 67
e-mail: directie@palm-nv.be
http://www.palm.be
Free tours available for groups of 15 to 45, Monday through Friday at 0900h, 1300h and 1800h (only 0900h Fridays). The tours, beginning with a trip on a small train, include a tasting.

Speciale Palm (Ale)
Steendonck (White)
Aerts 1900
Dobbel Palm (Special Noël)

Other sites

RODENBACH
Spanjestraat, 133
8800 Roeselare
Tel.: 051/22 34 00
Fax: 051/22 92 48
e-mail:
rodenbach@rodenbach.be
http://www.rodenbach.be
Free tours available including a tasting

Rodenbach (Flemish Brown)

Rodenbach Alexander (Flemish Brown)

Rodenbach Grand Cru (Flemish Brown)

RIVA

Wontergemstraat, 42
8720 Dentergem
Tel.: 051/63 36 81
Fax: 051/63 62 08

Dentergem Wit Bier (White)

Lucifer (Special)

Riva Pils (Pilsner)

St Arnoldus Triple (Abbey)

Other sites

LIEFMANS

Aalststraat, 200
9700 Oudernaarde
Tel.: 055/31 13 92
Fax: 055/31 94 86
Tours available year-round by appointment, price: 120 BEF including tasting. There is a small museum as well, in the heart of the brewery.

Liefmans Glühkriek (Flemish Brown)

Liefmans Frambozen (Flemish Brown)

Liefmans Goudenband (Flemish Brown)

Liefmans Kriek (Flemish Brown)

ROCHEFORTOISE

Rue du Theux, 43b
5580 Epraves
Tel.: 084/37 80 84
Fax: 084/37 84 45
e-mail:
brasserie@la-rochefortoise.com
http://www.la-rochefortoise.com
La Rochefortoise (blond & amber)

ROMAN

Hauwaart, 105
9700 Oudenaarde
Tel.: 055/45 54 01
Fax: 055/45 56 00
e-mail: globe@roman.be
Tours by appointment, price: 100 BEF including a tasting (free to school groups)

Romy Pils (Pilsner)
Ename Dubbel (Abbey)
Ename Tripel (Abbey)
Sloeber (Special)
Alfri (Pilsner)
Mater Wit Bier (White)

SILENRIEUX

Rue de Noupre s/n
5630 Silenrieux
Tel.: 071/63 32 01
Fax: 071/63 32 01
the Brasserie de Silenrieux is a very small brewery, founded by Eric Bedoret in 1992 on his parents' farm in the Ardennes. He recreates old, lost styles of beer, using locally grown special grains like spelt and buckwheat, and old local brewing recipes. The brewery also has a small bar and restaurant built in the same barn, where typical dishes, prepared with beer, are served. The brewery was one of the first Belgian establishments to brew organic beers.
Bière de l'Ours
Joseph Spelt Ale
Sara Buckwheat Ale

SILLY

Rue Ville Basse, 141
7830 Silly
Tel.: 068/55 16 95
Fax: 068/56 84 36
e-mail: contact@silly-beer.com
http://www.silly-beer.com
Group tours available by appointment, price: 100 BEF

Double Enghien Blonde (Special)
Double Enghien Brune (Special)
Saison de Silly (seasonal)
Scotch de Silly
Titje (White)

SINT-BERNARDUS
Trappistenweg, 23
8978 Watou
Tel.: 057/38 80 21
Fax: 057/38 80 71
e-mail: stbernwatou@hotmail.com
Tours available by appointment

St Bernardus Pater 6 (Abbey)
St Bernardus Prior 8 (Abbey)
St Bernardus Abt 12 (Abbey)
St Bernardus Triple (Abbey)

SINT-JOZEPH
Itterplein, 19
3960 Bree
Tel.: 089/86 47 11

Fax: 089/86 74 19
e-mail: bsj@st-Jozeph.be
Bokkereyer

SLAGHMUYLDER
Denderhoutembaan, 2
9400 Ninove
Tel.: 054/33 18 31
Fax: 054/33 84 45
Witkap Pater Tripel (Abbey)
Ambiorix (Special)
Helles (Export)
Slaghmuylder's Kerstbier (Special Noël)
Slaghmuylder's Paasbier (Easter Special)
Witkap Pater Dubbele (Abbey)
Witkap Pater Stimulo (Abbey)
The brewery displays a beautiful collection of antique brewing implements and old advertising posters. But the flower of the Ninove collection is a steam engine still in working order. Built in 1910, it was retired

from regular service in 1966 but can still, at appointed times, deliver all the power of its 60 horses.

STERKENS
Meerdorp, 20
2321 Hoogstraten
Tel.: 03/315 71 45
Fax: 03/315 94 20
e-mail: sterkens@tornado.be
St Paul Double (Abbey)
St Paul Triple (Abbey)
Kruikenbier (Special)
Poorter (Special)
St Paul Blond (Abbey)
St Paul Special (Abbey)
St Sebastiaan Dark (Abbey)
St Sebastiaan Grand Cru (Abbey)

STRUBBE
Markt, 1
8480 Ichtegem
Tel.: 051/58 81 16
Fax: 051/58 24 46
Houten Kop
Ichtegems (old brown)
Vlas Kop

TIMMERMANS JOHN MARTIN
Kerkstraat, 11
1701 Itterbeek
Tel.: 02/569 03 57
Fax: 02/569 01 98
Tours by appointment

Bourgogne des Flandres (Flemish Brown)
Timmermans Gueuze (spontaneous fermentation)
Timmermans Kriek *(cherry)* (spontaneous fermentation)
Timmermans Framboise *(raspberry)* (spontaneous fermentation)
John Martin (Ale)
Timmermans Cassis *(blackcurrant)* (spontaneous fermentation)

Timmermans Faro (spontaneous fermentation)
Timmermans Pêche *(peach)* (spontaneous fermentation)

VAL DE SAMBRE
Rue Vandervelde, 273
6534 Gozée
Tel.: 071/56 20 73
Fax: 071/56 20 74
Abbaye d'Aulne Blonde des pères (Abbey)
Abbaye d'Aulne Superbe (Abbey)
Abbaye d'Aulne Triple (Abbey)
Abbaye d'Aulne sur lie (Abbey)
Blanche de Charleroi (White)

VAN DEN BOSSCHE
St Lievensplein, 16
9550 Herzele
Tel.: 054/50 04 11
Fax: 054/50 04 06
Tours by appointment

Paterlieven Blond (Abbey)
Paterlieven Bruin (Abbey)
Lamoral Degmont (Special)
Van Den Bossche Kerstbier (Special Noël)

VAN EECKE
Douvieweg, 2
8978 Watou
Tel.: 057/38 80 30
Fax: 057/38 89 96
This independent family brewery traces its origins back to 1629, when, for the first time, a document mentioned that the local castle was adjacent to a brewery. During the French Revolution, the plundering French troops burned the castle and the brewery. Only the brewery was rebuilt by a local farmer in the same year of the destruction, under the slogan "Revolt all you want, but we still need beer here." Through marriage

"The John Martin's Finest Beers Selection":
An original range of special beers combining quality and tradition.
Developed with devotion since 1909 by the John Martin family business,
the selection puts the accent first on quality, then on diversity of
origin and strong individuality of taste.
From the John Martin's to the Gordon Finest Gold,
blond or dark, amber-coloured, fruity, sweet or slightly bitter,
the beers of the "John Martin's Selection" have always
fascinated beer lovers throughout the world.
We invite you to discover a unique range.
Taste and enjoy the experience.

the Van Eecke family became the owner of the brewery in 1862, where top fermenting country ales were brewed, but the brewery had only a local significance until well after WW II. With the revival of the authentic local ales in combination with TV and modern marketing in the 1960's, the delicious beers of the brewery became a hot commodity in bars and fine restaurants. The village of Watou is today part of the city of Poperinge, the heart of the last remaining area in Belgium where hops is cultivated.

Kapittel Abt (Abbey)
Kapittel Pater (Abbey)
Kapittel Prior (Abbey)
Poperings Hommel Ale
Witte Watou (White)

VAN HONSEBROUCK

Oostrozebeekstraat, 43
8770 Ingelmunster
Tel.: 051/33 51 60
Fax: 051/31 38 39
Brigand (Special)
Kasteelbier (Special)
Kasteelbier Tripel (Special)
St Louis Cassis *(blackcurrant)* (spontaneous fermentation)
St Louis Framboise *(raspberry)* (spontaneous fermentation)
St Louis Gueuze (spontaneous fermentation)
St Louis Kriek *(cherry)* (spontaneous fermentation)
Brigand Christmas (Special Noël)
Kasteelbier van Ooidonk (Special)

VAN STEENBERGE
(Ex BIOS)

Lindenlaan, 25
9940 Ertvelde
Tel.: 09/344 50 71
Fax: 09/344 54 20
http://www.vansteenberge.com

Tours available by written request during the tourist season, from 0930h to 1200h and 1430h to 1730h.

This independently owned family brewery is located in Ertvelde, North of Ghent, close to the Netherlands' border. The earliest written documents about the brewery date from 1784. Today the production stands at 40,000 barrels a year. The Van Steenberge beers are exported all over the world, and considered by the best known beer experts to be prize winning, top examples in their category. In the 1990's a state of the art automated brew-house and bottling installation was installed. Centuries old recipes, authentic craftsmanship, absolute quality and modern technology create some of the worlds best beers. It is one of only a few Belgian breweries that master the second fermentation in kegs, to create cask conditioned beers.

Augustijn (Abbey)
Augustijn Grand Cru (Abbey)
Bios Vlaamse Bourgogne
Bornem Double
Bornem Triple
Bruegel
Cherish Lambic
Corsendonk Pater (Abbey)
Gulden Draak (Special)
Piraat Triple IPA (Special)
Sparta Pils

VERHAEGHE

Beukenhofstraat
8570 Vichte
Tel.: 056/77 70 32
Fax: 056/77 15 61
Duchesse de Bourgogne
Vichtenaar

BROUWERIJ VAN STEENBERGE

The Art of Brewing perfected during 700 years

Authentic Belgian Abbey Ales
World class Triples
Amber & Bock
Lambics

"Living Beers"!

Quiz

1.What was the first beer brewed at Chimay in 1862?
a. Red 75cl
b. White 75 cl
c. Blue 75cl

2. The Chimay beers undergo a double fermentation. The first in the vat and the second
a. in oak barrels
b. in tanker lorry
c. in the bottle

3. By what name is the mixture of water, malt and cereals left in the vat after brewing known?
a. draff
b. boiled mash
c. wort

4. To what family does yeast belong?
a. bacteria
b. enzymes
c. mushrooms

5. Why is pilsner sometimes called "the little bohemian?"

6. Which is the patron saint on brewers?
a. St Augustin
b. St Arnold
c. St Eloi

7. Which of these breweries was at the same time a farm, a dairy and a bakery?
a. du Bocq
b. Dupont
c. Achouffe

8. What great Belgian poet said: "In our counties, the mayor is prince but the brewer is king?"

9. What vitamin is found in large quantities in most Belgian beers?

10. What is the peculiarity of the Het Anker à Malines brewery?
a. it is a steam brewery
b. it is a hanging brewery
c. it is a brewery without a brewer

11. In what sequence should a good bartender prepare this order: 2 draught beers, one abbey beer and 2 ports?

12. What are fermentation vats called?
a. the temples
b. the cauldrons
c. the vessels

13. What is the contents (volume) of a demi?

14. Who painted *The (beer) Drinkers (Les Buveurs)*?
a. Pierre Brueghel
b. Rubens
c. Frans Hals
d. Manet

15. Which of these four Brussels establishments is not situated on the Grand Place:
a. la Chaloupe d'Or
b. la Lunette
c. le Roy d'Espagne
d. la Brouette

16. Which was the first Belgian village granted the right to brew, by emperor Otto in 974?

17. Where do they exclusively serve sweet lambics in stoneware jugs?
a. at the Père Faro
b. at the Bécasse
c. at the Mort Subite

18. In what region is the greatest concentration of breweries found?
a. Charleroi
b. Courtrai
c. Louvain

19. How many litres of beer can be held in a pipe (cask)?

20. What are the large vats where the beer is stored after fermentation called?
a. tanks
b. chapels
c. guilloires

21. What spice lends the fruity flavors to Bush 7?

22. What gives beer its bitter flavor?
a. the hops
b. the kind of cereal used
c. the yeast

23. What is the minimum legal percentage of wheat that a lambic must contain?

24. What does not enter into the elaboration of the Hoegaarden white beer?
a. coriander
b. corn
c. orange zest
d. wheat

25. Which is called the beer of Bons Vivants?

a. Guillotine
b. Mort Subite
c. Delirium Tremens

26. In 1970, the Abbey Orval celebrated an anniversary. What venerable age had it reached?

27. Did king Léopold II have occasion to drink any Vieux-Temps?

28. In the time of the pharaoh Amenophis IV, what was the meaning of a dream involving beer?

29. The Toison d'Or is the name of a beer as well as an order of knights dating from the 13th century. Does the order still exist?

30. The Abbey of Affligem, which bequeathed to us a beer highly regarded today, was founded by:

a. six hermits

b. six bandits

c. six abbesses

Answers

1. Red 75cl

2. in the bottle

3. boiled mash

4. mushrooms

5. Because it comes from Bohemia (Czech Republic) where it was created in 1842

6. Saint Arnold

7. The Farm-Brewery Dupont à Tourpes

8. Emile Verhaeren (but many brewers combined the two roles)

9. Vitamin B, thanks to the yeast in the beer.

10. It is a hanging brewery (the brewing vats do not rest on the floor).

11. First the ports, the then abbey beer, and lastly the draught pilsners, poured at the last moment to ensure a good head.

12. Vessels (based on the word *vase*).

13. It means a glass with a volume equal to 25 centilitres

14. Frans Hals, but they all painted tavern scenes.

15. La Lunette, which is found near la Monnaie

16. The village of Liège, in order to oppose the supremacy of the church over the commerce of beer.

17. La Bécasse. These famous jugs measure from 0,5 litre to 15 litres.

18. Courtrai

19. A pipe is a cask of oak with a volume around 600 litres.

20. In the holding tanks.

21. coriander.

22. The hops

23. 30%

24. Corn

25. Mort Subite

26. Its 900th anniversary.

27. No. He died in 1909 and Vieux-Temps was created in 1935.

28. According to the book of dreams, dreaming of beer was a portent of happiness.

29. Yes. One of its most famous members is Juan Carlos, King of Spain.

30. They were six bandits who, in 1704, decided to make honorable amends and to begion their penitent life in Affligem.

BELGIAN BEER LOCATOR

Belgian Beer on the Internet

The Confederation of Belgian Breweries is one of the oldest professional associations in the world, but it doesn't prevent it from having a very modern website, *www.beerparadise.be*, where the beer lovers will find a lot of information about the Belgian breweries, which all belong to the Confederation. The site can be visited in English as well as in French or Dutch. But what if you're a real beer connoisseur but that you have trouble finding your favourite brands in your region, or that you simply don't want to spend too much time looking for them? The website *www.beerparadise.ltd.uk* offers brands from 30 different countries, particularly from Belgium, Germany and the United Kingdom

www.globalbeer.com will also provide you with lots of information about Belgian beer and the events having to do with it.. Last but not least, *www.belgianshop.com* specializes in Belgian beers (more than 600!) but also in Belgian chocolates, beer glasses and other objects connected with Belgian products. Even the Guide to Belgian Beers you're reading right now should be available there soon!

Belgian Beer Locator

Reading about beer is good, but drinking it is better. And you're lucky, since Belgium has plenty of places to do just that ! For each province, addresses have been separated into 3 categories ;

Museums : there are a dozen or more, each complementing

the others. Themes and contents vary according to their region. Some breweries have museums of their own, or offer for a modest sum, tours of their own facilities. Naturally, the tours end with a visit to the tasting room to sample one or more of the house beers (for more information see the section titled "Breweries").

From **Distributors to Boutiques** : Wholesale, agents and retail. These locations are the crucial intermediaries between the breweries (especially the smaller breweries) and the consumers. The choice can be overwhelming. Also check out the addresses in France and the Netherlands.

Cafés : We have selected those that present an large choice of beers, on tap or in the bottle. Local colour and flare, and a welcoming atmosphere often distinguish these places. They are worth the trip. As are the **restaurants** listed which specialize in recipes using beer (see "Brussels and Environs").

Antwerp

Museums

Brouwershuis
Adriaan Brouwersstraat, 20
2000 Antwerp
Tel.: 03/232 65 11
Open only by appointment
To see : Brewers House from the XVIth century

Agents and Boutiques

Belgium Beers
Reyndersstraat, 2
2000 Antwerp
Tel.: 03/226 68 53
Closed Tuesdays

Den Dorstvegel
Oude Vaartplaats, 12
2000 Antwerp
Tel.: 0486/71 79 12

't Brouwershuis
Molenstraat, 42
2387 Baarle-Hertog (Bar-Le-Duc)
Tel.: 014/69 94 03

Drankenhandel Van Oevelen
Moerkantsebaan, 47a
2910 Essen
Tel.: 03/667 23 06

Drinks Service
Dr Vandeperrestraat, 59a
2440 Geel
Tel.: 014/58 40 68

Db. Drinks Bavi
Nonnenstraat, 35
2800 Mechelen
Tel.: 015/20 36 65

Bierparadijs
Grensweg, 12c
2321 Meer
Tel.: 03/315 05 11

Albo
Struisbeeklaan, 10-12
2610 Wilrijk
Tel.: 03/449 99 10
Fax : 03/440 18 97

Cafés

De Cluyse
Oude Koornmarkt, 26
2000 Antwerp
Tel.: 03/232 35 16

Den Engel
Grote Markt, 3
2000 Antwerp
Tel.: 03/233 12 52

Kulminator
Vleminckveld, 32
2000 Antwerp
Tel.: 03/232 45 38

't Pakhuis
Vlaamse Kaai, 76
2000 Antwerp
Tel.: 03/238 12 40
Fax : 03/238 68 14

Pater Vaetje
Blauwmezelstraat, 1
2000 Antwerp
Tel.: 03/231 84 76

't Stamineeke
Vlasmarkt, 23
2000 Antwerp
Tel.: 03/231 96 72
Open from 1600h. Closed Tuesdays (and Wednesdays, October through May)

't Brouwershuis
Molenstraat, 42
2387 Baarle-Hertog (Bar-Le-Duc)
Tel.: 014/69 94 03

Den Grooten Wolsack
Wollemarkt, 16
2800 Mechelen (Malines)
Tel.: 015/21 86 03

In Den Spijtighen Dusel
Otterstraat, 99
2300 Turnhout
Tel.: 014/42 35 00

't Molenhuis
Antwerpsesteenweg, 378
2390 Westmalle
Tel.: 03/309 33 17
Closed Mondays and Tuesdays

Flemish Brabant

Museums

Musée de la Bière d'Abbaye
Abdijstraat, 8
1850 Grimbergen
Tel.: 02/269 46 72
Open 1000h to 1800h, Sundays 1400 to 1800h. Closed Wednesdays. Price : 100 BEF, including tasting (groups of 40 maximum : 150 BEF including guided visit, video presentation and tasting).
To see : This small museum holds information on Abbey brewed beers, ancient documents of the Prémontrés order, instructional explanations of brewing as well as a wide array of objects, all pleasantly presented. It is also possible, with prior arrangement, to reserve a private room accommodating up to 50.

Agents and Boutiques

Holemans

Langdorpsesteenweg, 117
3220 Aarschot
Tel.: 016/56 24 61

Dranken Neels

Aarschotsesteenweg, 4
3010 Leuven (Louvain)
Tel.: 016/23 20 63

Terclavers Drankservice

Mechelsestraat, 203a
3000 Leuven (Louvain)
Tel.: 016/20 20 00

De Bierschuur

Processiebaan, 3
1785 Merchtem-Peizegem
Tel.: 052/37 40 34

De Zennevallei

Wittouckstraat, 57-65
1600 Sint-Pieters-Leeuw
Tel.: 02/377 18 463

Woluwe Drink Service

Leuvensesteenweg, 566
1940 St-Stevens-Woluwe
Tel.: 02/720 04 17

Weynants

Weg Messelbroek, 154
3271 Scherpenheuvel
Tel.: 013/77 10 07

Wijns

Kerkstraat, 41
1742 Ternat
Tel.: 02/582 11 92

Cafés

De Kilo

Snassersweg, 46
1730 Asse

De Koekoek

Edwigsesteenweg, 200
1730 Asse
Tel.: 02/452 74 92

Sedan

Edwigsesteenweg, 200
1730 Asse

't Boske

Willem Eggerickxstraat, 7
1560 Hoeilaart
Tel.: 02/657 31 28
Closed Wednesdays

De Kring

Place Stevens Dewael, 15
1502 Lembeek
Tel.: 02/356 68 75
Closed Mondays

De Blauwe Kater

Hallengang, 1
3000 Leuven (Louvain)
Tel.: 016/60 05 80

Domus

Tiensestraat, 8
3000 Leuven (Louvain)
Tel.: 016/20 14 49

Nova

Kerklaan, 19
1830 Machelen
Tel.: 02/252 04 87
Closed Wednesdays

Merchtemse Poort

Nieuwstraat, 2
1785 Merchtem
Tel.: 052/37 21 58
Closed Wednesdays after 1200h

In de Oude Huis van Mekingen

J.B. Cardijnstraat, 10
1600 Sint-Pieters-Leeuw
Tel.: 02/356 19 74

't Vlaamsch Huis

Steenhuffeldorp, 29
1840 Steenhuffel
Tel.: 052/30 00 47
Open after 1200h. Closed Saturdays and Sundays

The flat country: the land of beer

Narixa
Hoornzelstraat, 67
3080 Tervuren
Tel.: 02/767 42 74
Closed Mondays

In't Vagevuur
Vlezenbeeklaan, 91
1602 Vlezenbeek
Tel.: 02/377 89 20

In't Verdiep
Postweg, 63
1602 Vlezenbeek
Tel.: 02/569 33 06

Wisemaele
Steenweg op Nieuwrode, 28
3111 Wezemaal
Tel.: 016/58 11 46
Closed Tuesdays

West Flanders

Museums

Musée Brugeois de la Malterie et de La Brasserie
Verbrand Nieuwland, 10
8000 Brugge (Bruges)
Tel.: 050/33 06 99
Fax : 050/33 46 44

Open from 1400h to 1800h, from the 1st of May to the 30th of September. Closed Mondays and Tuesdays. Price : 100 BEF, including tasting (groups accommodated with notice).
To see : The brewing museum *De Gouden Boom* is located in the old brewery and malting house that closed its doors in 1976. Open since 1991, it includes most notably information on different barley malting methods, historic breweries of Bruges and a café from 1900.

Musée National Du Houblon
Gasthuisstraat, 71
8970 Poperinge
Tel.: 057/33 40 81
Fax : 057/33 57 03
Open from the 1st of July to the 15th of September, from 1400h to 1800h, Sundays and holidays in May, June and September (by arrangement for groups from the 15th of March to the 1st of November).
To see : In an ancient hops warehouse and drying building, the "king" of the

region is presented through numerous photos and panels, explaining its cultivation and methods of use.

Agents and Boutiques

Bis

Doorniksesteenweg, 272
8580 Avelgem
Tel.: 056/64 83 30
Fax : 056/64 83 40

Bottle Shop

Wollestraat, 13
8000 Brugge (Bruges)

Huis Cosaert Freddy

Markt, 35
8000 Brugge (Bruges)
Tel.: 050/33 39 35

Message in a Bottle

St Amandstraat, 21
8000 Brugge (Bruges)
Tel.: 050/33 75 51

Woolstreet

Wollestraat, 31
8000 Brugge (Bruges)
Tel.: 050/34 84 44

Ter Posterie Winkel

Rijselstraat, 57
8900 Ieper (Ypres)
Tel.: 057/20 05 80

Supermarkt Roby

Hoornwerk, 44
8930 Menen (Menin)
Tel.: 056/51 28 14

Vladis

Groentenmarkt, 3
8400 Oostende (Ostende)
Tel.: 059/70 81 39

Cuvelier Noel

Abelestationplein, 30
8970 Poperinge
Tel.: 057/33 33 05

Delicia

Rumbeeksesteenweg, 323
8800 Roeselare (Roulers)
Tel.: 051/20 09 42
Closed Tuesdays

Yves Streekbieren

Onze-Lieve Vrouwmarkt, 1
8800 Roeselare (Roulers)
Tel.: 051/22 21 88
Closed Wednesdays and Sundays after noon

Le Palais de la Bière

Leiestraat, 11
8940 Wervik
Tel.: 056/.31 17 11

Bierwinkel Bacelle

Roeselarestraat, 47
8560 Wevelgem
Tel.: 056/41 21 31
Fax : 056/42 34 76

Rotsaert

Remiclaeysstraat, 28
8210 Zedelgem
Tel.: 050/20 94 98

Cafés

't Brugs beertje

Kemelstraat, 5
8000 Brugge (Bruges)
Tel.: 050/30 96 16

De Brugse Bierkaai

Nieuwstraat, 9
8000 Brugge
Tel.: 050/34 38 00
Fax : 050/33 35 32

Den Dijver

Dijver, 5
8000 Brugge (Bruges)
Tel.: 050/33 60 69

Erasmus

Wollestraat, 35
8000 Brugge (Bruges)
Tel.: 050/33 57 81
Closed Mondays and from 15/01 to 15/02

De Garre

De Garre, 1
8000 Brugge (Bruges)
Tel.: 050/34 10 29

De Torre

Memling laan, 2
8420 De Haan
Tel.: 059/23 65 32

't Rusteel

Heulestraat, 168
8560 Gullegem
Tel.: 056/35 65 64
Open Thursdays, Fridays, Saturdays and Mondays from 1500h; Sundays from 1400h to midnight. Closed Tuesdays and Wednesdays.

Schildia

Zeedijk, 250
8301 Heist
Tel.: 050/51 50 58

Posterie

Rijselstraat, 57
8900 Ieper (Ypres)
Tel.: 057/20 05 80

De Brouwzaele

Kapucijnenstraat, 19
8500 Kortrijk (Courtrai)
Tel.: 056/20 25 33
Open every day except Mondays, from noon to 0300h

't Mouterijtje

Kapucijnenstraat, 25a
8500 Kortrijk (Courtrai)
Tel.: 056/20 14 14

Botteltje

Louisastraat, 19
8400 Oostende (Ostende)
Tel.: 059/70 09 28

't Ostens Bierhuis

Kapucijnenstraat, 48
8400 Oostende (Ostende)
Tel.: 059/70 67 01
Open from 1400h. Closed Tuesdays.

Café de la Paix

Grote Markt, 20
8970 Poperinge

Flandria

Grote Markt, 30
8630 Veurne (Furnes)
Tel.: 058/31 11 74
Open from 0900h. Closed Thursdays.

East Flanders

Museums

Musée de la Bière

Kuipstraat, 36
9940 Ertvelde
Tel.: 09/344 81 47

To see : Since 1992, Rémi and Bérénice Dheane display more than 3700 different beers, from more than 100 countries. Visitors will discover in addition, an un-equaled collection of glassware, coasters and advertising materials.

Agents and Boutiques

Vandenameele

Meistraat, 4
9300 Aalst (Alost)
Tel.: 053/70 38 15

Vandevoorde

Hoge Kouter, 20
9880 Aalter
Tel.: 09/374 23 24

Stravbier

Parochiestraat, 4
9472 Denderleeuw
Tel.: 053/66 72 25

Maes Etienne Industrieterrein

Hoogveld, 29
9200 Dendermonde (Termonde)
Tel.: 052/21 53 69

De Hopduvel
Coupure links, 625
9000 Gent (Gand)
Tel.: 09/225 20 68

Vandermolen Jos
Poortakkerstraat, 19
9051 Gent (Gand)
Tel.: 09/221 34 41

Bierhalle
Hovenierstraat, 36a
9230 Melle
Tel.: 09/330 88 44

Sandersput
Brusselsteenweg, 333
9400 Ninove
Tel.: 054/32 99 66

Geers
Ledergemstraat, 7
9040 Oostakker
Tel.: 09/351 05 83

Drink Center Deriemaeker
Bruneellaan, 11
9600 Ronse (Renaix)
Tel.: 055/21 99 63
Fax : 055/21 99 63

Drink Party Center
Industriepark – Noord, 35
9100 Sint-Niklaas
Tel.: 03/776 53 55

Dirk Verstraete
Patronagestraat, 22
9060 Zelzate
Tel.: 09/345 74 44

Cafés

Augustijn
Markt, 82
9800 Deinze
Tel.: 09/387 78 10

De Heeren van Liedekercke
Kasteelstraat, 33
9470 Denderleeuw
Tel.: 053/68 08 88
Open from Thursdays through Mondays

In 't Schippershuis
Scheldekant, 19
9070 Destelbergen
Tel.: 09/228 03 49
Closed Mondays and Tuesdays

Brouwzaele
Ter Platen, 17-19
9000 Gent (Gand)
Tel.: 09/224 33 92

De Dulle Griet
Vrijdagmarkt, 50
9000 Gent (Gand)
Tel.: 09/224 24 55

Hopduvel
Rokerelstraat, 10
9000 Gent (Gand)
Tel.: 09/225 37 29

De Tempelier
Meersenierstraat, 9
9000 Gent (Gand)
Tel.: 09/225 17 40
Open every day except Wednesdays

Waterhuis aan de Bierkant
Groentenmarkt, 9
9000 Gent (Gand)
Tel.: 09/225 06 80

St Tropez
Brabantdam, 164
9000 Gent

Velootje
Kalvertsteg, 2
9000 Gent

De Presse
Markt, 50
9500 Geraardsbergen (Grammont)
Tel.: 054/41 69 24
Open Thursdays through Sundays

Saf
Stationplein, 13
9500 Geraardsbergen (Grammont)
Tel.: 054/41 24 02

Schuttershof
Dendermondsesteenweg, 79
9280 Lebbeke
Tel.: 052/41 43 24

The House of Brewers, which still houses the Federation of Brewers (CBB) and the Museum of Brewing Industry.

Hot Te Puttens
Wichelsestraat, 22
9340 Lede
Tel.: 053/80 51 30
Open Fridays, week-ends and holidays

Rembrandt
Heerweg, 29a
9667 Sint-Maria-Horebeke
Tel.: 055/45 61 77

Grouwesteen
Grouwesteenstraat, 19
9170 Sint-Pauwels
Tel.: 03/776 66 06

De Muze
Beislovenstraat, 4
9620 Strijpen
Tel.: 09/360 69 04

Bloemenlust
Smetledstraat, 61
9230 Wetteren
Tel.: 09/369 10 30
Open only week-ends except July through August

Zwarte-Fles
Joachim-Schayckstraat, 2b
9052 Zwijnaarde
Tel.: 09/221 53 35
Closed Mondays and Tuesdays

Barrels of gueuse beer

Limburg

Museums

Bocholter Brouwerijmuseum
Dorpstraat, 53
3950 Bocholt
Tel.: 089/46 34 24
Fax : 089/46 34 24
Open from 1300h to 1700h Wednesdays, Fridays and weekends from the 1st of July to the 30th of September (and all year to groups of 20 or more). Price : 175 BEF.

To see : Considered by its owners to be one of the largest in Europe, the Musée de la Brasserie Martens had its doors opened in 1979 by Jean Martens. It retraces the different steps of the brewing process with materials from several countries : Belgium, Germany and Great Britain. In 1997, a new wing was added to the existing building. There visitors will discover two brewing rooms, fermentation vats, a micro-brewery, merry-go-round and several vehicles used at the brewery. Diverse package deals are offered in collaboration with local restaurants and children can take advantage of a play area specifically for them.

Agents and Boutiques

Steyfkens
Hasseltweg, 363
3600 Genk
Tel.: 089/35 25 82
Closed Mondays

Dranken Dalemans
Bungalowpark, 1b
3940 Hechtel-Eksel
Tel.: 011/73 40 93
Fax : 011/73 36 85

Pauwels
Kloosterstraat, 71
3920 Lommel
Tel.: 011/54 43 62

Corstijns – Vinken
Rijksweg, 13
3630 Maasmechelen
Tel.: 089/75 62 55
Fax : 089/75 20 92

't Bakske
Hulsterweg, 47
3980 Tessenderlo
Tel.: 013/66 10 77

Cafés

Defl Ure Mis
Kardinaal Mercier Straat, 23
3200 Aarschot
Tel.: 016/69 69 25

Hemelrijk
Hemelrijk, 11
3500 Hasselt
Tel.: 011/22 28 51

De Wedelse Molen
Breugelweg, 250
3900 Overpelt
Tel.: 011/63 22 47
Open from 1200h

Taverne Haspengouw
Sint-Genovevaplein, 8
3800 Sint-Truiden
(Saint-Trond)
Tel.: 011/68 59 78

Paenhuys
Schorterweg, 1
3980 Tessenderlo
Tel.: 013/66 52 21

Madrigal
St Maternuswal, 8
3700 Tongeren
Tel.: 012/23 88 45

Brussels and surroundings

Museums

Musée de la Brasserie C. B. B.
Grand'Place, 10
1000 Bruxelles
Tel.: 02/511 49 87
Fax : 02/511 32 59
http://www.beerparadise.be

e-mail : cbb@beerparadise.be
*Open every day from 1000h to 1700h. Closed 25/12 and 01/01.
Price : 100 BEF per person inclu-*

**Grand'Place, 2-3
Tél 02/511 54 94**

ding tasting (75 BEF for groups, free to school groups).

To see : Under the world's most beautiful city square, the museum showcases brewing which respects tradition, but uses modern techniques. All steps of the process are shown, there are numerous screens of information and tasting of one of the member brewery beers.

Musée Schaerbeekois de la Bière

Avenue Louis Bertrand, 33
1030 Bruxelles
Tel.: 02/216 59 70
Open Wednesday and Saturday from 1400h to 1800h

To see : The museum has reconstructed an ancient brewery using materials from the Roelants brewery, the last of 15 breweries in Schaerbeek to produce Kriek in the 19th century, which closed its doors in 1956. Over 100 bottles of beer, all Belgian, are on display, as well as posters and enameled plaques. The Rocs Abbey Brewery (Hainaut) brews a beer for the museum, available for tasting in the pub.

Musée Bruxellois de la Gueuze

Rue Gheude, 56
1070 Bruxelles
Tel.: 02/520 49 28

Fax : 02/520 28 91
Open Monday through Friday, from 0830h to 1700h, Saturday from 1000h to 1700h. Closed Sunday and holidays. Price : 100 BEF per person, including tasting and guide service (groups : 1500 BEF maximum, 50 BEF children under 12 years, 90 BEF 12 to 18 years). Guided visits by reservation only.

To see : This centenarian brewery (Cantillon) has housed since 1978 a museum of Gueuze which has only grown in reputation : the 300.000 mark for international visitors should be reached this year. Here you will find, in addition to the museum itself and observation of production, expositions with diverse themes (notably, corkscrews in the Spring of 2000) organized regularly. A "Brasserie Portes Ouvertes" (Open Door Brewery) event is held several times a year, during which the public is welcomed from 0630h to 1700h and may follow the different stages of brewing. Possibility of a light meal with preliminary reservation.

Agents and Boutiques

Bier Tempel
Rue du Marché aux Herbes, 56
1000 Bruxelles
Tel.: 02/502 19 06

Délices et Caprices
Rue des Pierres, 51
1000 Bruxelles
Tél. : 02/512 14 51

Drinks Delepine Yves
Rue Eugène Cattoir, 13
1050 Ixelles
Tel.: 02/640 45 64
Fax : 02/640 36 23

Belle-Vue
Rue Delaunoy, 58
1080 Molenbeek Saint-Jean
Tel.: 02/412 44 11
Closed weekends

Cafés

La Bécasse
Rue de Tabora, 11
1000 Bruxelles
Tel.: 02/511 00 06

Au Roy d'Espagne
Grand' Place, 1
1000 Bruxelles
Tel.: 02/513 08 07

Le Bier Circus
Rue de l'Enseignement, 89
1000 Bruxelles

La Brouette
Grand'Place, 2-3
1000 Bruxelles
Tél. : 02/511 54 94

Le Corbeau
Rue Saint-Michel, 20
1000 Bruxelles
Tel.: 02/219 52 46

Béguines des Béguines

Rue des Béguines, 168
1080 Brussels

Tel./Fax : 02 414 77 70

Cuisine based on beer

L'Ecuyer
Rue de l'Ecuyer, 3
1000 Bruxelles
Tel.: 02/219 90 99

L'Imaisge Notre-Dame
Rue Marché-aux-Herbes, 8
1000 Bruxelles
Tel.: 02/219 42 49

Laploc
Rue de l'Ecuyer, 29
1000 Bruxelles

La Lunette
Place de la Monnaie, 3
1000 Bruxelles
Tel.: 02/218 03 78

La Mort Subite
Rue Montagne-aux-Herbes-Pota gères, 7
1000 Bruxelles
Tel.: 02/513 13 18

The Chatterbus

The not-for-profit organization "The Chatterbus" (The Bavard Bus) is an original initiative to say the least, trying to make people more familiar with Brussels. It is all about guided tours, original and convivial, for groups. Organised either in busses – as the name indicates – or on foot, they try to show Brussels from an angle other than what is seen in the never-ending rotation of the Grand'Place – Manneken Pis – Atomium. Themes as diverse as Art Nouveau, Brussels in Comic Strip and the Marolles are offered. Of course, we can't keep quiet about the trip entitled "The Review of Belgian Beers". It exists in two different versions : an "aperitif" version and a "gastronomic" version. The first familiarises you with the brewing world, Belgian in general, and Brussels' in particular. The second is accompanied by a meal in which each of the dishes is made with beer as a base ingredient. As for the trip entitled "What the Pubs Tell About Brussels", it focuses on, as you might have guessed, the old cafés, whether they are popular or upscale. Two thirst quenching stops are planned.

Bus Bavard – rue des Thuyas, 12 – 1170 Brussels – Tel. 02/673.18.35 – Fax. 02/675.19.67 – www.busbavard.be – e-mail : busbavard@skynet.be

Poechenellekelder

Rue du Chêne, 5
1000 Bruxelles
Tel.: 02/511 92 62

La Porte Noire

Rue des Alexiens, 67
1000 Bruxelles

Le Vieux Chateau d'Or

Rue Sainte-Catherine, 26
1000 Bruxelles
Tel.: 02/513 31 26

L'Atelier

Rue Elise, 77
1050 Ixelles
Tel.: 02/649 19 53

Chez Moeder Lambic

Rue de Savoie, 68
1060 Saint-Gilles
Tel.: 02/539 14 19

Restaurants

Generally, those restaurants with specialties on their menu using beer also have other classic Belgian specialties, and vice versa.

Drie Fonteinen

H. Terlinckplein, 3
1650 Beersel
Tel.: 02/331 06 52
  rabbit à la gueuze, vinaigrette and vinegar of lambic,...

Le Paon Royal

Rue du Vieux Marché aux Grains, 6
1000 Bruxelles
Tel.: 02/513 08 68
  veal à la Kriek, cod à la blanche (white beer),...

La Rose Blanche

Grand' Place, 11
1000 Bruxelles
Tel.: 02/513 64 79
  salmon à la faro, filet of lamb à la Gauloise,...

In 't Spinnekopke
Place du Jardin-aux-Fleurs, 1
1000 Bruxelles
Tel.: 02/511 86 85
carbonnades à la lambic, scallops Saint-Jacques à la Trappiste de Rochefort

Le Miroir
Place Reine Astrid, 24-26
1090 Jette
Tel.: 02/424 04 78
carbonnades à la faro

La Béguine des Béguines
Rue des Béguines, 168
1080 Molenbeek Saint-Jean
Tel.: 02/425 77 70
scampi with endive and gueuze, sausage from Fagnes en croûte with goat's cheese and coulis of tomato with Orval, rabbit loin with rosemary and Trappiste de Chimay

Les Trappistes
Chaussée de Gand, 408
1080 Molenbeek Saint-Jean
Tel.: 02/411 90 89
burbot à la blanche (white beer), scampi in pastry à la St Feuillien,...

Walloon Brabant

Agents and Boutiques

Choppin Michel
Chaussée de Huy, 98
1325 Dion-Valmont
Tel.: 010/68 92 50
Fax : 010/68 95 90

DD Drink
Rue de l'Artisanat, Zone Industrielle Sud
1400 Nivelles
Tel.: 067/84 15 38

Cafés

Le Rétro
Avenue Fernand Charlot, 2
1370 Jodoigne
Tel.: 010/81 03 42

La Podo
Avenue Albert et Elisabeth,
1400 Nivelles
Tel.: 067/21 21 68

L'Arrêt du Temps
Rue de Mons, 133
1480 Tubize
Tel.: 02/355 50 59

Café de Paris
Chaussée de Bruxelles, 199
1410 Waterloo
Tel.: 02/354 08 44
open from 1030h

Hainaut

Agents and Boutiques

Ponselet
Route de Mons, 56
6150 Anderlues
Tel.: 071/52 50 41

Primevères Drive In
Zoning Les Primevères
7800 Ath
Tel.: 068/28 77 77

Ets Decoster
Place du Belvédère
6570 Beaumont
Tel.: 071/58 95 65

A l'Orgerie
Place Ste Anne, 14
7780 Comines
Tel.: 056/55 49 05

Brasserie Brouta
Rue de Fontenelle, 2
6240 Farciennes
Tel.: 071/81 01 11

Le Drink de la Gare
Route de Bavay, 74
7040 Genly
Tel.: 065/56 82 61

Drink Bultia
Rue Neuve, 69
6280 Gerpinnes
Tel.: 071/22 03 56

Car Drink 2000
Rue de la Station, 8
7973 Grandglise
Tel.: 069/56 08 58

Sandras
Route d'Ath, 246
7050 Jurbise
Tel.: 065/22 99 45
Fax : 065/22 80 26

Mouscron Drink Market
Rue de la Marlière, 19
7700 Mouscron
Tel.: 056/34 54 52

Galerie BDJ
Grand'Rue, 143
7700 Mouscron
Tel.: 056/84 70 78

Vanuxeem
Rue d'Armentières, 150
7781 Ploegsteert
Tel.: 056/58 89 23
Fax. : 056/58 75 59
Open Monday to Thursday from 0900h to 1200h and 1330h to 1900h; Friday and Saturday from 0900h to 1900h

Le Palais de la Bière
Rue de Roubaix, 40
7520 Templeuve
Tel.: 069/35 21 85

Delaby Boissons
Rue Dorez, 8
7500 Tournai
Tel.: 069/84 00 92

Drink Shop
Rue de la Frontière, 39b
7380 Quiévrain
Tel.: 065/46 51 31

Quiévrain Drink
Rue de Mons, 143
7380 Quiévrain
Tel.: 065/46 51 40

Cafés

Au fil de l'eau
Chaussée de Terre, 77
7800 Ath
Tel.: 068/28 33 28

Auberge du Passe Tout Outre
Rue Chevauchoir, 1
7387 Autreppe
Tel.: 065/75 90 59
Open from 1100h. Closed Monday

L'Auberge de Poteaupré
Rue de Poteaupré, 5
6464 Bourlers
Tel.: 060/21 14 33

Open everyday 1100h to 2200h. Closed Monday in off-season

La Fermette des Pins
Rue du Lustre, 39
7133 Buvrinnes
Tel.: 064/34 17 78
Open Thursday to Monday, inclusive

La Cuve à Bière
Boulevard Jacques Bertrand, 68
6000 Charleroi
Tel.: 071/32 68 41

Aux Mille Colonnes
Rue de Marchienne, 6
6000 Charleroi
Tel.: 071/32 05 34

Rhumerie Le Corto
Rue de Montigny, 12
6000 Charleroi
Tel.: 071/32 02 32

Les Templiers
Place du Manège, 7
6000 Charleroi
Tel.: 071/32 18 36

Le Relais de la Ronce
Place des Comtes, 12
7191 Ecaussinnes
Tel.: 067/48 58 60

L'Enseignement
Chaussée de Boulinsart, 34
6060 Gilly
Tel.: 071/48 81 13

Au Rapieur
Grand Place, 14
7000 Mons

La Cervoise
Grand Place, 25
7000 Mons

Le Greffier
Grand' Place, 16
7000 Mons
Tel.: 065/31 16 80

La Maison des Brasseurs
Grand' Place,4
7000 Mons
Tel.: 065/35 18 28

Le Podo
Rue de la Coupe, 43
7000 Mons
Tel.: 065/34 70 77

Belle-Vue
Rue du Curé, 4b
7542 Mont-Saint-Aubert
Tel.: 069/22 88 65
Closed Monday through Thursday and in February

La Belle Epoque
Grand Place
7700 Mouscron

Café de l'Ours
Rue de Tourcoing, 72
7700 Mouscron
Tel.: 056/33 04 87

Café de Paris
Rue de Valenciennes, 116
7380 Quiévrain
Tel.: 065/45 14 63

Chez Tintin
Rue Masse-Diarbois
6043 Ransart
Tel.: 071/35 84 78

No Comment!

Here are a few extracts from the "Manuel du Soiffard" (Drinker's Manual), sub-titled the Bar Survival Guide, which points out certain excellent (?) reminders to the more enthusiastic among you. Attention... *"ce n'est pas de la petite bière!"*

Symptom : feet cold and wet.

Cause : glass held in the incorrect position.

Action : turn the glass so that the open end is pointing at the ceiling.

Symptom : beer bizarrely colourless and without flavour.

Cause : your glass is empty.

Action : find someone to buy you another round.

Symptom : wall opposite is covered with neon tubes.

Cause : you've fallen on your back.

Action : re-attach yourself to the bar.

Symptom : beer without taste, the front of your shirt is wet.

Cause : mouth closed, or glass held up to incorrect location on the face.

Action : go to the toilettes, practice in front of the mirror.

Symptom : feet hot and wet.

Cause : loss of control of your evacuation system.

Action : go to the nearest dog and complain about his manners.

Symptom : the floor is swimming.

Cause : you are looking through the bottom of your empty glass.

Action : find someone to buy you another round.

Symptom : the floor is shaking.

Cause : you are being carried by others.

Action : find out if they can take you to another bar.

Symptom : the room seems especially dark.

Cause : the bar is closed.

Action : ask the barkeeper for you address.

Le des Ombiaux

Place du Chapître, 1
6530 Thuin
Tel.: 071/59 42 12
Closed Sunday in the off-season

Le Bouchon

Quai du Marché aux Poissons, 23
7500 Tournai
Tel.: 069/21 54 36

La Cave à Bière

Quai Taille-Pierres, 3a
7500 Tournai
Tel.: 069/21 29 45
Open Thursday to Sunday

Le Moine Austère

Rue Dorez, 5
7500 Tournai
Tel.: 069/84 21 30
Closed Monday

The Province of Liège

Museums

Musée de la Biere et du Pékêt

Avouerie d'Anthisnes
Rue de l'Abbaye, 19
4160 Anthisnes
Tel.: 04/383 63 90
Open the 1st of April to the 15th of September, Tuesday to Sunday, from 1200h to 1800h (to 1700h Tuesday and Thursday); the 16th of September to the 31st of March, from Monday to Friday, 1100h to 1800h (to 1700h Tuesday and Thursday). Closed January, except to groups of 20 or more. Price : 115 BEF including admission to the chateau, museum and tasting (85 BEF for children

and 105 BEF/ person for groups).

To see : The museum focuses on the discovery of flavour. 250 types of Belgian beers are indexed and classified. Glassware, bottles, distilling materials and antique posters are presented in separate rooms. Another room, more instructional, serves to explain the aromas produced during the steps of the brewing process.

Agents and Boutiques

Drink Piron
Rue de Battice, 93
4880 Aubel
Tel.: 087/68 70 29

Stassen
Place Albert Ier
4880 Aubel
Tel.: 087/68 63 66

Brasserie Makart
Rue Jean Vololers, 68
4340 Awans
Tel.: 04/363 51 54

Caves de Xheneumont
Xheneumont, 1a
4651 Battice
Tel.: 087/67 42 96

Drinx & Co
Route de Herve, 104 bis
4651 Battice

Drinx & Co
Aachenstrasse, 62
4700 Eupen

Hesby Drink
Rue de Landen, 61
4280 Hannut
Tel.: 019/51 61 11
Fax : 019/51 60 31

Bollinne
Avenue des Fossés, 36
4500 Huy
Tel.: 085/23 19 69
Fax : 085/21 40 22

Ludo Drink
Chaussée de Tongres, 460
4000 Liege – Rocourt

Brasserie Coune
Chaussée Romaine, 57
4360 Oreye
Tel.: 019/67 70 81

Brasserie Delbrouck
Rue de la Vallée, 10
4410 Saint-Georges
Tel.: 04/259 70 50

Brasserie Salmon – Magnee
Avenue des Lanciers, 105
4900 Spa

Boulanger Dominique
Avenue René Lange, 114
4910 Theux – Jehonster
Tel.: 087/23 08 79

Toby Drink Market
Rue P. Michaux, 76
4683 Vivegnis
Tel.: 04/364 10 72

Mondial Drinks
Rue Lavaniste Voie, 162
4041 Vottem
Tel.: 04/227 92 92

Brasserie Casthy
Rue de Visé, 747
4020 Wandre
Tel.: 04/362 61 34

Cafés

Le Vaudrée
Rue du Val Benoît, 109
4031 Angleur
Tel.: 04/367 10 61

Au Vieil Aubel
Rue de Battice, 2
4880 Aubel
Tel.: 087/68 71 40

La Fontaine Gauloise
Rue de la Fontaine, 7
4260 Avennes
Tel.: 019/69 99 38

A surprising museum…

Les Jardins d'Amélie
Chaussée de Namur, 13
4210 Burdinne
Tel.: 081/83 41 27
Closed Monday

Les Roches
Rue de la Station, 10
4130 Esneux
Tel.: 04/380 23 00

Au Grain d'Orge
Centre, 16
4852 Hombourg
Tel.: 087/78 77 84
Closed Tuesday

Big Ben
Grand Place, 8
4500 Huy
Tel.: 085/23 15 83

Alt Kelmis
Rue de Liège, 196
4720 La Calamine
Tel.: 087/65 81 07

As Quinquet
Rue St Folien, 6
4020 Liège

Au Fût
Rue Louvrex, 1
4000 Liège
Tel.: 04/222 33 10
Closed Monday

La Pierre Levée
Rue de Serbie, 62
4000 Liège
Tel.: 04/252 35 60

Le Saint-Paul
Rue Saint-Paul, 8
4000 Liège
Tel.: 04/223 72 17
Closed Sunday

Le Vaudrée II
Rue Saint-Gilles, 149
4000 Liège
Tel.: 04/223 18 80

Les Caves à Bière
Place Kuborn, 4
4100 Seraing
Tel.: 04/337 94 84

't Boerenhof
De Plank, 24
3790 Sint-Martens-Voeren
Tel.: 04/381 23 33

Brasserie de la Plume
Rue de l'Egalité, 476
4630 Soumagne
Tel.: 04/377 52 37

Vieilles Caves d'Artois
Avenue F. Nicolay, 7
4970 Stavelot
Tel.: 080/86 20 17

The Kings Head Inn
Dorpsstraat, 9
3793 Teuven-Voeren
Tel.: 04/381 13 24

La Taverne de Trooz
Grand Rue, 254
4870 Trooz
Tel.: 04/351 66 71
Closed Thursday night and Wednesday

La Boule Rouge
Pont Saint Laurent, 10
4800 Verviers
Tel.: 087/33 39 50

The Province of Luxembourg

Agents and Boutiques

Dispa
Route de Bomal, 42a
6940 Barvaux-Sur-Ourthe
Tel.: 086/21 11 24

Le Pré Vert
Rue du Sablon, 105
6600 Bastogne
Tel.: 061/21 28 48

Le Marché de Nathalie
Grand' Rue, 22
6830 Bouillon
Tel.: 061/46 89 40

Confiture St Amour
Place des Récollets
6940 Durbuy

Drink Market Destine
Rue des Ecoles, 71
6990 Hotton
Tel.: 084/46 68 57

Interboissons
Rue Albert1er, 95
6810 Pin-Izel

Cafés

Taverne de la Brasserie
Achouffe, 32
6666 Achouffe
Tel.: 061/28 94 55

Brasserie Lamborelle
Rue Lamborelle, 19
6600 Bastogne
Tel.: 061/21 80 55

La Vieille Ardenne
Grand' Rue, 9
6830 Bouillon
Tel.: 061/46 62 77

Le Jacquemart
Rue Simon, 1
6990 Hotton
Tel.: 084/46 61 10

Le Vénitien
Rue de l'Eglise, 28
6980 La Roche en Ardenne
Tel.: 084/41 16 37

Le Lion Rouge
Galerie Chantercy (Place de la Gare)
6800 Libramont
Tel.: 061/22 57 26

Yes
Grand Rue, 70
6800 Libramont

le Miami
Place du Marché, 27
6870 Saint Hubert
Tel.: 061/61 13 83

L'Escale
Avenue de la Salm, 1
6690 Vielsam
Tel.: 080/21 41 30

Auberge de l'Ange Gardien
Rue de l'Abbaye
6823 Villers-Devant-Orval
Tel.: 061/31 18 86
Open weekends, from February through November; everyday from the 15th of March to the 15th of October

The Province of Namur

Museums

Musée des Bières Belges
Rue de la Gare, 19
5170 Lustin
Tel.: 081/41 11 02
Fax : 081/41 37 66
Open from 1100h to 1930h every day from the 1st of July to the 31st of August, and weekends and holidays from the 1st of September to the 30th of June (also by appointment for groups). Price : 60 BEF.

Gambrinus Drivers Museum
Rue Fontaine St Pierre, 2a
5660 Romedenne
Tel.: 082/67 83 48
Fax : 082/67 83 48
Open from the 1st of April to the 1st of November, every weekend from 1100h to 1900h; every day in July and August. Price : 170 BEF (100 BEF/person for groups)
To see : A unique museum, housed in an ancient brewery and malting house and dedicated to brewery vehicles of all ages. A monument to the memory that, until 1930, breweries were the largest market for lorry makers. The museum has 20 vehicles, and 50 cases of other diverse objects, all gathered by the brewing phenomenon that is Charles Fontaine.

Agents and Boutiques

Balleux
Route de Rochefort
5570 Beauraing
Tel.: 082/71 14 14

Michaux
Chaussée d'Yvoir, 1a
5500 Dinant
Tel.: 082/22 48 05

Sandron
Rue du Monastère, 2
5644 Ermeton Sur Biert

Poncelet
Route de Charleville, 72
5575 Gedinne
Tel.: 061/58 85 54

La Cave de Wallonie
Rue de la Halle, 6
5000 Namur
Tel.: 081/22 06 83
Open Tuesday to Saturday inclusive

Scaillet
Parc Industriel
5580 Rochefort
Tel.: 084/22 11 21
Fax : 084/22 13 27

Ets Hallet
Rue Reine Elisabeth, 12
5081 St Denis Bovesse
Tel.: 081/56 60 73

Cafés

Moulin de Kevret
Rue de Haillot, 153
5300 Andenne
Tel.: 085/84 49 33
Open Thursday and Friday from 6pm to 11pm and from 12am to 11pm on week-ends.

Le Sax
Place Reine Astrid, 13
5500 Dinant
Tel.: 082/22 51 66

Pichet du Père Marlet
Rue Lespagne, 48
5540 Hastiere-Lavaux
Tel.: 082/64 51 60
*Open weekends and holidays all year;
every day in July and August.*

Café Musée des Bières Belges
Rue de la Gare, 19
5170 Lustin
Tel.: 081/41 11 02

Le Bouffon du Roi
Rue de Bruxelles, 60
5000 Namur
Tel.: 081/22 33 82

Le Chapitre
Rue du Séminaire, 4
5000 Namur
Tel.: 081/26 04 90

La Malle Poste
Rue de Behogne, 46
5580 Rochefort
Tel.: 084/21 09 86
Closed Wednesdays

Larger Shops

Not withstanding the almost inexhaustible diversity of the boutiques, there has recently been an expansion of the "Beer" selection in the larger shops. This follows partly from the increased popularity of specialty beers, but also from the "local effect" that is revolutionizing other super market departments as well. Generally, the larger brands are available in all countries, while the regional, or lesser known are available in the stores of their home region. Cora and Delhaize, principally, have developed a virtual politics of local beers.

Colruyt
153 stores, various locations.

Cora
5 stores in the Walloon region and 2 in Brussels, around 150 different brands.
This chain developed a system for promotion of specialty beers and has regular sales. Cora organizes a festival of beer in February and September.

Delhaize
115 supermarkets "Le Lion" and 120 "AD Delhaize", 174 brands distributed locally and 84 making up a national "basket". Delhaize "regionalizes" Belgian beers.

GB
(232 "super" and 57 "maxi"). The GIB group offers a more classic, though nonetheless interesting selection.

Super M
6 stores. Here one finds the ubiquitous specials as well as the traditional pilsners. At times, sales provide the opportunity to buy packages of bottles + glassware.

Belgian Beer Locator for The Netherlands

Alambic
Hoogstraat, 139-141
3111HE Schiedam
Tél. : 076/522 83 94

Astein
't Hoogvelt, 6
5721VW Asten
Tél. : 0493/69 37 86

Bieren en Pintelieren
Pasqualinistraat, 2
5622AW Eindhoven
Tél. : 040/243 54 22
Fax. : 040/243 54 22

De Biergigant
Van Goorstraat, 5
4811HH Breda
Tél. : 076/522 83 94

't Bierhuys
Gasthuislaan, 40
2611RB Delft
Tél. : 015/213 40 47
Fax. : 010/411 28 79

't Bierhuys
Hoogstraat, 66a
3011PT Rotterdam
Tél. : 010/411 24 96
Fax. : 010/411 28 79

De Bierkoning
Paleisstraat, 125
Amsterdam
Tél. : 020/625 23 36
Fax. : 020/627 06 54

De Bier Wereld
Molenweg, 261
6543VE Nijmegen
Tél. : 024/373 28 20
Fax. : 024/373 19 16

De Bierwinkel
Asselstraat, 26a
7311EM Apeldoorn
Tél. : 055/522 48 55

Burg Bieren
Putterweg, 45
3851GB Ermelo
Tél. : 0341/56.49 34
Fax. : 0341/55 99.22

Hansen Dranken
Veestraat, 6
6067AS Linne
Tél. : 0475/46 53 00

Hennie Berendsen
Deuringerstraat, 27
7514BC Enschede
Tél. : 053/431 52 64

't Koelschip
Grotemarkt, 211
1315JE Almere Stad
Tél. : 036/530 06 14
Fax. : 036/545 06 21

De Kruis
Lagedijk, 13
1544BA Zaandijk
Tél. : 075/640 11 10
Fax. : 075/640 11 12

De Man van Drank
Hartesteeg, 13
Leiden
Tél. : 071/512 28 13
Fax. : 071/512 28 13

Schuermans
Veldhovenring, 60
5041BD Tilburg
Tél. : 013/543 08 72

Van Erp
Grote Kromme Elleboog, 16
9712BK Groningen
Tél. : 050/312 64 14
Fax. : 050.313 93 24

Wijn & Bier Boutique
Leyweg, 803-805
2545HA Den Haag
Tél. : 070/366 70 92

Woudenberg
Junusstraat, 55-59
6701AX Wageningen
Tél. : 0317/41 23 01
Fax. : 0317/42 43 64

Belgian Beer Locator for the United Kingdom

Scotland and Northern Ireland

Fencebay Fisheries
Fairlie
KA29 0E Ayrshire

Oast's and Toast
107-109 Morrison Street
EH3 HBX Edinburgh

The Vineyard
375/377 Ormeau Road
BT7 3GP Belfast

Northern England & Isle of Man

Beers in Particular
151 Highgate, Kendal
LAS2AT **Cumbria**

Binns
House of Frazer
High Row, Darlington

Corbridge Larder
Hill Street
NE45 5AA **Corbridge, Northumberland**

Glenridding Mini Market
Glenridding
CA11 0PA **Ulswater, Penrith**

McClouds
Harbour View, Roker Pier

Roker, Sunderland

The Vineyard
10 Malew Street
IM9 1AB **Castletown, Isle of Man**

Wells Wine Cellar
94-100 St Thomas Street
YO11 1DU **Scarborough**

Manchester, Liverpool, North West England and North Wales

Bottle Stop
136 Acre Lane
SK8 7PD **Bramhall, Stockport**

Pick a Flick
89 Crosby Road
L23 STD **Crosby, Liverpool**

Rainhall Drinks Company
18-22 Rainhall Road
BB18 5AF **Barnoldswick**

Thirst for Beer
Unit 2 Y'Maes
LL53 5HA **Pwllheli, Gwynedd**

Vins de Bordeaux
63 George Street
OL1 1LX **Oldham**

The Whisky Chaser
30 St. Annes on Sea
FY8 1QR **Lancashire**

Yorkshire and North Eastern England

Beer Paradise
Yorkshire Mill Village
Batley, West Yorkshire

Beer Ritz
Market Square
HG5 8AL **Knaresborough, North Yorks**

Beer Ritz
Victoria Buildings, Weetwood Lane
LS16 5LX **Far Headingly, Leeds**
Tél. : 0113/275 34 64

Beer Ritz
31 Stone Gate
YO1 8AW **York**
Tél. : 0190/464 43 44

Houlton Cash and Carry
1 Maltings Way, Market Street
DN3 32DH Grimsby,
Lincolnshire

McClouds
Hardwick Road
Pontefract

Rythm & Booze
140 Boothferry Road
Goole

Rythm & Booze
11 Wesley Street
Osset, **Wakefield**

The Midlands and South Wales

Cambridge Wine Merchants
2 Mill Road
CB1 2AD Cambridge

Discount Supermarket
97-99 Whitechurch Road
CF14 3JP Cardiff

Rackhams
Corporation Street
Birmingham

Stirchley Wines and Spirits
1533/37 Pershore Road
B30 2JH Stirchley,
Birmingham

Weavers Way Wine Cellar
The Old Hall, Bickling Road
MR11 6ND Aylsham, Norfolk

London and the South

Army and Navy
101 Victoria Street
SW1 6QX London

Cave Direct
Unit 5A, Larkfield Trading Estate, Hythe Lane
ME20 6SW Larkfield, Kent
Tel.: 0162/271 03 39

Message in a Bottle
66 Fore Street
EX3 0HL Topsham, Exeter, Devon

Palmer Wines
61 Workingham Road
RG6 1LH Reading

Selfridges, Wines and Spirits
Oxford Street
W1A 1AB London

Wycombe Wines
20 Crendon Street
HP13 6LS High Wycombe, Bucks

Belgian Beer Locator for the United States

Some states like Ohio, Georgia, the Carolina's, etc., discriminate against good beer. They allow wine and hard liquor into the State, but they don't allow beer of a certain alcohol content. Write to your state representatives and ask them to stop the discrimination.

Other states like Vermont, Utah, Iowa, etc., have monopolized the sale of beer over a cer-

Between England and Belgium... a true love story

The takeover of the British groups Whitbread and Bass by Interbrew is the latest evidence of a long and beautiful love story between Belgium and England. We can in fact imagine that it started in 1524 when the Flemish brought the culture of hops to the island. But the reciprocity is equally viable. To whit, the official magazine of the Confederation of Belgian Brewers (C.B.B.) was founded by the Englishman George Maw Johnson in 1893. English soldiers, during the First World War, passed along their habit of consuming beers like « Pale Ale » and « Scotch », which encouraged the Belgian brewers to make their own. But the 100% Belgian example of English influence is without a doubt Orval. This beer uses a cold hopping process – giving it a particular bitterness – as is practiced in England.

tain alcohol content. Only the state store can sell it, or retailers have to buy it from the state. These authorities try to keep as many brands as they can out of the state. The good news is that the state has the obligation to bring in your favorite brand when you insist upon your rights.

June 2001 and the state of Florida still keeps European style bottle sizes out, and insist on a US size of 8 or 12 oz. Write to your state representatives and ask them to stop the discrimination.

In most liberated states every retailer, every restaurant and every pub with a liquor license can stock your favorite brands. It's entirely up to the retailer to buy that brand from the whole-saler. Put the retailer to work for you and get the brands you want.

Agents and Boutiques

Arizona

Chandler: AJ's Fine Food. *Mesa*: Sun Devil Liq. *Tempe*: Claim Jumper, Timberwolf, Old Chicago. *Tucson*: Smith's Food.

California

Many cities: Whole Foods Markets, Trader Joe's, Beverages & More. *Albany*: Solano Cellars. *Atwater:* Perry's pub. *Boulder Creek*: New Leaf Market. *Capitola*: 41st Ave Liquors. *Clovis:* BC's Pizza. *Costa Mesa*: Hi Time Cellars. *Cayucos*: Hoppe's Garden Rest. *Downey*: Brewers Rendez-Vous. *Escondido*: Holiday Wine Center. *Fresno:* Body & Bog, Old Doc's Liq. *Glendale*: Red Carpet. *Huntington Beach:* Liquor Warehouse. *Irvine*: Ant Hill Pub. *Long Beach*: Morry's of Naples, Yardhouse, Wine country. *Los Altos*: Draegers. *Los Angeles*: Wine House, Beverage Warehouse, Newsroom. *Menlo Park*: Beltramo's. *Modesto:* The Wine shop. *Orange*: Hollingshead Deli. *Ojay*: Ojai Liq. *Palm Springs*: Rest. Pomme Frite. *Pasadena*: Lucky Baldwin. *Redondo Beach*: Naja's. *San Diego*: Fair Liq., Henry's, Clems' Bottle House. *San Francisco*: Lucky 13 Bar, Caruso Wine, Slanted Door, Cannery Wine, Lulu, Toronado. *San Gabriel*: Stuffed Sandwich. *San Juan Capistrano*: Rest. L'Hirondelle. *San Luis Obispo:* Sandy's Deli. *Santa Barbara*: Dutch Garden Restaurant, San Roque Liquors, Bouchon Rest. *Santa Monica*: Library Ale House, Wine Expo, Matisse. *Seal Beach*: The Abbey. *Sonoma*: Wine Exchange. *Visalia:* Franks Liq., Urban Gourmet,Vintage Press Rest.

Colorado

Boulder: Harvest Wine, Liquor Mart, Ace Discount. *Denver*: Falling Rock, Mundo Vino. *Fort Collins*: Pringles Fine Wine. *Lakewood*: Union Liq. *Littleton*: The Wine Company. *Louisville*: Superior Liq. *Thorton*; Total Beverage.

Florida

Clearwater: World of Beers. *Napels:* London Pub. *Sarasota*: Cock-&-Bull Bar. *Tampa:* Tampa Bay Brewery, Barley Hoppers, Brewshack. *Temple-Terrace:* Beverage Castle.

Georgia

Athens: Five Points Bottle. *Atlanta:* Brickstore pub, Harry's Farmers market, Greens. *Augusta:* Harvard Wine & Spirits. *Cumming:* Taco Mac. *Duluth:* Kurt's Restaurant. *Sandy Springs:* Taco Mac. *Savannah:* Haversham Beverage. *Snelleville:* Taco Mac *Warner Robins:* Bootleggers.

Iowa

Iowa City: John's Grocery. *Ames*: Cyclone Liquors.

Illinois

Many cities: Whole Foods Markets. *Chicago*: Jake's Pub, Sam's Wine, Shaefer's, Quencher's, Delilah's, Maproom.

Indiana

Greenwood: John's. *Indianapolis*: Chalkies Bar, John's, Kahn's fine wine, Tarkington's. *Porter*: Pat's Liq., Wagner's Ribs. *Valparaiso*: Triangle Liq., Wagner's Rib, Pastimes.

Kentucky

Bellevue: Party Source. *Covington*: Cork & Bottle. *Louisville*: Party Source, Bristol Barn & Grill.

Kansas

Wichita: Maryott Wine, Jacob Liq.

Maine

Biddeford: Coastal Discount, Bradbury Bros. *Lewiston*: Saunders Village. *Pemiquid*: Colonial Pemiquid Tavern. *Portland*: RSVP, Mazza, Market Wines. *Rockland*: Contes. *Rockport*: The Market Basket. *Saco*: Vic & Whits. *Waterboro*: JD'S Package Store. *Wells*: Tully's Beer & Wine. *Windham*: Leaf & Bean. *Wiscasset*: Treats.

Maryland

Aberdeen: Short Stop Liq. *Annapolis*: Griffin's, McGarveys, Middletons. *Baltimore*: Wells Liq., Wild Mushroom, Café Tatoo. *Bethesda*: Sutton Place Gourmet. *Catonsville*: Super Cut Rate Liq. *Elkton*: State Line Liq. *Forest Hill*: Ronnies. *Frederick*: Westside Disc. Liq., Ye Old Spirit Shop. *Hagerstown*: Washington Spy. *Ocean City*: Ollie's pub. *Olney*: Le Manneken pis. *Parkville*: Liquor Pump.

Massachusetts

Allston: Sunset Bar & Grill. *Boston*: Marty's, Martignetti's, Blanchards, *Cambridge*: Wine Cheese Cask. *Chelmsford*:

Harringtons. *Marlboro*: Julio's. *Medford*: Kappy's. *Newton:* Marty's. *Quincy*: Richards. *Saugus*: Kappy's. *Somerville*: Downtown Liquors. *Sudbury*: Kappy's.

Minnesota
Burnsville: Blue Max Liq. *Minneapolis:* Broviak Liq., France 44 Liq., South Lyndale Liq., Surdyk's Liq. *St. Paul:* Cellar's Wine, Haskell's Wine, 1st Grand Liq.

Michigan
Ann Arbor: Ashley's, Big Ten. *Berkley*: Berkley Front. *Dearborn:* Merchants Warehouse. *Detroit:* Centre Street Café. *East Pointe:* Merchants Warehouse. *Grosse Pointe:* Cadieux Cafe. *Royal Oak:* Merchants Warehouse. *Wyandotte:* Oak Café, Discount Drinks.

Missouri
Richmond Heigths: Starr's. *University City:* Cicero's.

New Jersey
Bordentown: Grapevine Lounge. *Bridgeport*: Logan Liq. *Brigantine*: Ocean Beverage. *Cherry Hill*: The Spirit Shop. *East Windsor*: Carduner's Liq. *Egg Harbor*: Joe Canal's Liq. *Elm*: White Horse Liq. *Ellwood*: Coffee's Tavern. *Haddonwood*: Haddonwood's Liq. *Hammonton*: Clark's Discount. *Hainesport*: Canal's Discount Liq. *Lindenwold*: Pike Liq. *Malaga*: Little Ease Tavern. *Marlton*; Canal's Liq. *Mays Landing*: Mill Street Liq. *Medford*: Harry's Liq. *Mercerville*: Shop Rite Bar, Glendale Liq. *Millville*: Buy Rite, City Liq., Lalli's Liq., Paper Waiter Pub. *Mt. Holly*: Liquor Fair, Liquor Loft. *Mt. Laurel*: Martin's Liq. *Pennington*: Circle Package. *Pennsauken*: Canal's Discount.

Penns Grove: Inky's Discount. *Princeton*: Princeton Wine. *Rocky Hill*: Towne Wine. *Sewell*: Moore's Liq. *Somers Point*: Pearl Rest. *Stockton*: Philip's Liq. *Swedesboro*: King's Liq. *Trenton*: Cedar Gardens Rest., H.K. Discount, Grillo's pub, Lanmark, De Forte's Rest. *Vineland*: William's Liq., Lincoln Liq., Clarks Discount, Ingram's. *Voorhees*: Voorhees Liq. *West Deptford:* Liquor Gallery. *Wiliamstown*: Canal's Liq. *Yardville*: Old Yardville Hotel.

New York
Brooklyn: Thrifty American, Cobble Heights Beverage. *Buffalo*: Pizza Plant. *New York City*: Markt, Belgo, DBA, Burp Castle, Waterloo, Deli Plus, Fancy grocery, Dean & Deluca, Happy Deli, Pioneer, Café de Bruxelles. *Queens*: Beverage Wagon, Cyprus Deli. *Staten Island*: Champ Beverage. *Syracuse*: Blue Tusk, McGregor's, Clark's, Party Source.

Ohio
Akron: Mustard Seed Market. *Bexley*: Bexley's Monk. *Cincinnati*: Wild Oats. *Cleveland Heights*: Cleveland Co-op. *Columbus*: Grapes of Myrth, Anderson, Wild Oats. *Euclid*: Warehouse Beverage. *Fairfield*: Jungle Jim's. *Lakewood*: Rozi's Wine House. *Mariemont*: Dilly Deli. *Solon*: Mustard Seed Market. *Springfield*: Wine Works. *Toledo*: Anderson.

Oregon
Eugene: Cornocopia Bottling. *Oregon City*: Bridgeview beer. *Portland*: Burlingame Market, Belmont Station, Higgins Rest., Horse Bras Pub, Bridge Port Ale House, Snake & Weasel,

Suzie O'Conell Market, Nature's stores. *Seaside*: Wine Haus.

Pennsylvania

Bridgeville: Burgh's pizza. *Crafton*: Sharp Edge Creek House. *Emmaus*: Shangy's. *Exton*: Drafting Room. *Fallston*: Black Door Tavern. *Homestaed*: Chiodo's tavern. *King of Prussia*: Watson, Kunda. *Mckees Rocks*: Tony Savatt. *Moon:* The Trivia Pub. *Newtown*: Isaac Newtons. *Philadelphia*: Monk's Café, Khyber Pass, Bridgid's, Cuvee Notre Dame, Foodery, Friedland, Stone's Beer, Bell Beverage, Latimer Deli. *Pittsburgh*: Sharp Edge Beer Emporium **(Best Belgian beer bar in the USA: 40 Belgians on tap!!! Always.)**, D's 6-pax, Fathead's, Smokin Joe's, Roland's, Mellinger. *Spring House:* Drafting Room. *Wayne*: The beverage store.

Tennessee

Brentwood: Brentwood Wine. *Clarksville*: Merchants. *Cookeville*: Bud's Lounge, Pub 32. *Franklin*: Cool Springs Wine. *Murfreesboro*: The Boro. *Nashville*: MacDoogals Liq., Midtown Wine, Nashville Wine, Mr. Whiskers, J. Barleycorn, West Meade Liq., The Beer Seller, Boscos, The Boundry, Flying Saucer, Broadway Brew House, Eddie's George's Place

Texas

Austin: Central Market,Whole Foods, Gingerman, Crown & Anchor, The Belgian Rest, Draught Horse, Whip-In. *Houston*: Spec's Liquor, Whole Foods, Gingerman, Flying Saucer. *Dallas*: Whole Foods, Gingerman, Flying Saucer. *Fort Worth*: Flying Saucer. *San Antonio*: Hill's and Dale's, HEB Foods.

Virginia

Cities: Fresh Fields Markets. *Blacksburg*: Vintage Cellars. *Chantilly*: Total Beverage. *Charlottesville*: Market Street Wine shop. *Occoquan*: Bistro Belgique Gourmande. *Vienna*: Norm's Beer & Wine.

Washington DC

Whole Foods Market, Cairo Liquors, Chevy Chase Wines, Brickskeller, The Saloon.

Washington State

Seattle: the Stumbling Monk, Bottle Works.

Wisconsin

Appleton: Flanagan. *Bookfield*: Market Basket. *Green Bay*: Woodman's, Campa's Wines. *Madison*: Woodman's, Steve's Liq. *Manitowoc*: Van's Liq. *Mequon*: Grapes & Wines. *Milwaukee*: Discount Liquors, Mader's Restaurant. *Wauwatoso*: Ray's Liquor.

Little lexical

Ale:
an English style beer, light, made with roasted hops.

Aroma:
odorous emanation from certain vegetable and animal substances; odour; perfume.

White:
a pale yellow beer, cloudy, originally from the Hoegaarden region and flavoured with coriander and orange peel.

Brasserie:
a brewery, from the Celtic word braces meaning germinated barley, that is, malt.

Cervoise:
barley fermented in water.

Double:
a beer with a crude extract ratio at least twice the average for the category. This can be obtained by either raising the quantity of primary solid materials (malt, hops,...) or by using a smaller amount of water. " Doubles " generally have very dark colour and caramel flavour. They are found principally among the Trappist and Abbey beers.

Faro:
a light beer, made with the addition of sugar and blended lambics, produced in the region of Brussels.

Fourquet:
a wooden tool used in the past to stir the mixture of malt and water. It was shaped like a large pierced spoon and was abandoned with the arrival of the industrial age.

Taste:
one of the five senses, thanks to which we discern flavours. The organs of taste are the taste buds, found on the tongue; they discern only the four basic flavours: salt, sweet, bitter and acid.

Gruyt:
a mixture of herbs and aromatics that preceded the discovery and use of hops. The Bishop-Prince Notger (Principality of Liège) saw fit to mandate a "Gruytrecht", the right to deal in gruyt, conferred by Otto the First.

Gueuze:
a beer composed of Lambics of different ages. Spelled geuze in Dutch.

Hops:
an aromatic plant of which the flowers of the female excrete lupulin, a substance that flavours most beers.

Hectolitre:
100 litres, by definition. Brewery production as well as export figures are always expressed in hectolitres.

Kilning (see Roasting)

Lambic or lambiek:
a beer produced in Belgium, made with malt and raw wheat by spontaneous fermentation.

Lupulin:
a yellow-gold powder contained in the un-pollinated female flowers of the hops plant. The principle aroma of beer.

Malting:
an operation consisting of germinating raw barley (or any other grain) by soaking it in water.

Pilsner:
a bottom fermented beer, originated in the village of Pilsen or Plzen (Czech Republic).

Roasting (or Kilning):
a procedure consisting of drying and aromatisation, via hot air, of the raw, germinated malt. It is also during this stage, which may last 20 to 48 hours, that the malt will develop its colour and specific flavour, mostly thanks to a final high heating or "coup de feu". (synonym: Kilning)

Saccharometre:
an instrument for saccharometry.

Saccharometry:
the practice of measuring the quantity of sugars dissolved in a liquid.

Saccharomyces:
the yeast that produces alcoholic fermentation of liquefied sugars, used in the production of wine, beer, ciders, etc.

Trappist:
a Belgian beer, produced in one of the 6 monasteries that obey the rules of the Cistercian order of Trappist monks.

Triple:
a beer with a crude extract ratio at least three times the average for the category (see Double). They are generally clearer than " doubles ", sometimes almost blond and always have higher alcohol content.

Beer is nourishing

INDEX

C

D

E

F

G

H

I

J

K

L

M